CORPORATE MAHABHARATA

NAVIGATING CORPORATE THROUGH THE LENS OF GREATEST INDIAN EPIC

ARNAB BASU

Made with ♥ on the Notion Press Platform
www.notionpress.com

CORPORATE MAHABHARATA

NAVIGATING CORPORATE THROUGH THE LENS OF GREATEST INDIAN EPIC

ARNAB BASU

Made with ♥ on the Notion Press Platform
www.notionpress.com

To My Heart & Home

Contents

Contents

Contents

Introduction

Overview of the Mahabharata

The Mahabharata, an epic written in ancient India, stands as one of the longest literary works in history, comprising roughly 100,000 verses or about ten times the length of the Iliad and the Odyssey combined, and is often attributed to the sage Vyasa, who is said to have composed it in the 4th century BCE, although its narratives likely evolved over centuries prior to this formal compilation. Set primarily within the context of the Kurukshetra region, the epic revolves around the dynamic and often tumultuous relationships between two families—the Pandavas and the Kauravas—who are embroiled in a relentless conflict marked by themes of ambition, power, and duty, offering profound insights into human nature and ethical dilemmas. The narrative is structured into 18 books known as Parvas, each revealing different facets of the story, including intricate subplots and moral discourses, making it a treasure trove of philosophical wisdom. The beginning, Adi Parva, introduces the principal characters such as the Pandavas—Yudhishthira, Bhima, Arjuna, Nakula, and Sahadeva—and the Kauravas, led by the enigmatic Duryodhana, setting the stage for future conflicts. The saga unfolds through multiple phases: the game of dice that leads to the Pandavas' exile, their return, and the subsequent war that culminates in the devastating battle of Kurukshetra. The epic's exploration of dharma—the moral and ethical duty of individuals—serves as a central theme, intricately woven into the characters' struggles as they navigate personal desires against societal expectations. The dialogue between Arjuna and Krishna, particularly as depicted in the Bhagavad Gita, becomes an essential philosophical component, elucidating complex ideas about righteousness, selflessness, and the nature of existence—an essential guide for individuals grappling with their own moral choices. The characterization within the Mahabharata is notably rich and multifaceted; figures like Draupadi, who embodies strength and agency, challenge traditional gender roles, while Karna, a tragic hero loyal to his friends yet torn between his sense of duty and identity, evokes sympathy and complexity. The epic is not merely a historical or literary document; it is a philosophical treatise that delves into issues of justice, loyalty, and the complexities of human relationships, emphasizing that the pursuit of power can lead to catastrophic consequences, as portrayed in the tragic aftermath of the Kurukshetra War. Many lessons regarding leadership, ethics, and collaboration are drawn from the trials and tribulations experienced by its characters—depicting the significance of teamwork exemplified by the bond of the Pandavas, who, despite their individual strengths and weaknesses, exhibit unity in adversity. Additionally, notable figures such as Bhishma, the grand patriarch representing unwavering loyalty and sacrifice, alongside the divine intervention of Krishna, who serves as a guide and counselor to Arjuna, encapsulate the roles of wisdom and guidance in ethical decision-making. So monumental is the Mahabharata's impact that its themes resonate throughout contemporary society, emerging in discussions surrounding morality, governance, and ethics, demonstrating the timeless nature of its teachings as they apply to the modern corporate and personal realms, urging individuals to reflect on the righteousness of their choices and actions. Ultimately, the Mahabharata serves as a comprehensive and enduring source, continuously inviting readers to engage with its multifaceted narratives, enriching the understanding of life's moral complexities while providing a narrative canvas that reflects not only the cultural ethos of ancient India but also timeless human conditions that remain relevant across generations. Its enduring legacy is found not just within the bounds of literature but in the fabric of ethical considerations within society, confirming the epic's role as both a mirror of ancient values and a beacon guiding contemporary discourse on morality.

Themes and characters

The Mahabharata, one of the most significant literary works in ancient India, encapsulates a vast array of themes and characters that delve deeply into the intricacies of human existence, morality, and society. At its core, the epic revolves around the saga of two families—the Pandavas and the Kauravas—whose rivalry ultimately culminates in the catastrophic war of Kurukshetra. Dharma, or righteousness, stands as the overarching theme, where characters are often faced with moral dilemmas that challenge their understanding of duty and justice. Each character in the Mahabharata embodies a unique interpretation of dharma, affecting their choices and the broader narrative arc. For instance, Yudhishthira, the eldest Pandava, is often portrayed as the epitome of truthfulness and moral integrity, yet his commitment to dharma leads to his downfall in the game of dice, illustrating the complex interplay between ethical conduct and situational consequences. Conversely, Bhima, renowned for his physical strength, represents the theme of loyalty and emotional depth, particularly in his unwavering support for his brothers and his fierce defense of their honor. Arjuna, the central figure and a master archer, epitomizes the internal conflict of facing moral questions on the battlefield, especially in his famous dialogue with Krishna in the Bhagavad Gita, where he grapples with the implications of warfare against his kin, emphasizing the profound philosophical discourse surrounding duty and selflessness. Central to the narrative is Krishna, who serves as Arjuna's charioteer and divine guide, embodying the concept of divine intervention in human affairs and offering essential teachings on life, duty, and righteousness that transcend the immediate context of the epic. On the opposing side, figures like Duryodhana, the eldest Kaurava, represent ambition and the darker aspects of power. His character highlights the consequences of unchecked desire and hubris, which severely impact his moral compass and eventually lead to the devastation of the war. The presence of Draupadi, the wife of the Pandavas, introduces themes of femininity, strength, and resilience, as she navigates her own trials, including the public humiliation she suffers at the hands of the Kauravas, challenging societal norms and expectations of women in her time. Moreover, characters like Karna, whose tragic fate evokes empathy, explore themes of loyalty and the search for one's identity amidst the chaos of familial allegiance and societal judgment, as he remains devoted to Duryodhana despite knowing the moral implications of his choices. The Mahabharata also intricately weaves in the theme of Karma, highlighting the belief that every action has significant consequences, reflected in the fate of each character. The epic's philosophical depth is further enriched by secondary characters such as Bhishma, the patriarch who embodies the principles of sacrifice and loyalty but faces the tragic consequences of his vows, and Vidura, who represents wisdom and moral integrity, often serving as a voice of reason amidst the corruption surrounding him. The relationships among characters also deepen the exploration of human emotions, showcasing the complexities of love, jealousy, betrayal, and forgiveness. The diverse cast of characters speaks to the intrinsic values of familial loyalty and rivalries, emphasizing how human connections are often fraught with conflicting desires and ethical commitments. Literary critics and scholars have noted how the Mahabharata is not merely a story of good versus evil; rather, it presents a nuanced portrayal of human nature, where virtuous characters can falter and flawed individuals exhibit moments of profound wisdom and bravery. As such, the Mahabharata serves as both a historic narrative and a timeless reflection on the moral dilemmas faced by individuals, making its themes—of dharma, karma, and the complexity of human emotion—perennially relevant across generations. The epic is rich with philosophical dialogues, especially in the Bhagavad Gita, capturing the essence of existential questions and the human condition, inviting readers to reflect upon their own lives and decisions in the light of dharma. Hence, the characters of the Mahabharata epitomize the rich tapestry of Indian culture, ethics, and philosophy, ensuring its status as a foundational text that informs contemporary thought on morality, governance, and personal conduct. Ultimately, the Mahabharata masterfully intertwines its themes and characters to explore the nature of duty, the impacts of choice, and the quest for truth in a world where human desires often clash with moral imperatives, proving that the dilemmas faced by its characters are timeless reflections of the perennial struggle between right and wrong, love and hate, and the pursuit of justice in a complex world.

The significance of the Mahabharata in Indian culture

The Mahabharata holds a profound significance in Indian culture, embodying the complexities of human nature, ethical dilemmas, and philosophical inquiries that resonate through centuries, shaping the moral and cultural fabric of society. As one of the longest epics in the world, it transcends mere storytelling to serve as a foundational text that influences literature, art, politics, and spirituality in India. The narrative of the Mahabharata explores fundamental themes such as duty (dharma), righteousness, justice, and the consequences of actions, making it a timeless reference for ethical conduct and decision-making. Central to its significance is the concept of dharma, which not only dictates the characters' actions but also provides a framework for understanding one's responsibilities within society. The epic presents the characters, particularly the Pandavas and Kauravas, as embodiments of various human virtues and vices, prompting readers and audiences to reflect on their own lives and the moral choices they face. This duality allows the Mahabharata to serve as a mirror for society, encouraging introspection and a deeper understanding of human behavior. The dialogues and discourses within the epic, especially those involving Lord Krishna, convey profound philosophical insights, addressing existential questions and the nature of reality, which continue to inspire philosophical and theological discourse in modern India. Furthermore, the Mahabharata has significantly influenced various art forms, from classical dance and theatre to modern adaptations in films and television, thus reaching diverse audiences across different mediums and generations. It has inspired countless retellings and interpretations, each adding layers to its already rich narrative tapestry, showcasing its adaptability to contemporary contexts while retaining its core messages. The epic's characters, particularly figures like Draupadi and Karna, resonate deeply within the cultural consciousness, representing ideals of resilience, justice, and compassion, thereby serving as role models for various aspects of life. The Mahabharata also addresses the concept of the "just war" (Dharma Yudhha), providing a discourse on the ethical implications of conflict that remains relevant in discussions of modern warfare and international relations, underscoring the need for ethical considerations in times of strife. Moreover, its teachings on governance and leadership provide timeless lessons for contemporary political leaders, advocating for integrity, wisdom, and empathy in the exercise of power. In the context of social justice, the Mahabharata challenges caste and gender norms, particularly through the character of Draupadi, whose plight raises questions about women's rights and societal roles, fostering discussions that remain pertinent in today's dialogues on gender equality. As a cultural touchstone, the Mahabharata reinforces the interconnectedness of history, mythology, and philosophy, allowing individuals to draw upon its teachings to navigate the complexities of modern life. In educational settings, it serves as a critical tool for imparting moral values, encouraging students to engage with ethical questions and the consequences of their choices. Additionally, the Mahabharata's festivals and rituals, celebrated across India, reinforce communal bonds and cultural identity, creating shared experiences that bind people together. Its narratives are invoked in spiritual practices, with verses recited for guidance and reflection, illustrating the epic's integration into daily life and its role in shaping spiritual beliefs. Overall, the Mahabharata is not merely an ancient text but a living tradition that continues to evolve, adapting its timeless messages to address the challenges and realities of contemporary society, ensuring its place as a cornerstone of Indian culture that influences generations to come.

Relevance of Mahabharata to Modern Business

The Mahabharata, an ancient Indian epic, offers a treasure trove of insights and lessons that resonate profoundly with modern business practices, ethical dilemmas, leadership strategies, conflict management, and decision-making frameworks. Central to the narrative are themes of duty (dharma), justice, and ethical behavior, which echo the core values that contemporary organizations strive to uphold. The concept of dharma in business emphasizes the importance of adhering to moral principles while pursuing profit, underlining that success should not come at the cost of ethical compromises. In an age where corporate governance and social responsibility have become paramount, lessons from the Mahabharata reinforce the idea that businesses must act responsibly towards all stakeholders, including employees, customers, and the community at large.

Moreover, the Mahabharata explores the complexity of human emotions and relationships, which are critical in navigating the modern business landscape characterized by teamwork and collaboration. The dialogues between characters like Krishna and Arjuna illustrate the importance of guidance, mentorship, and communication, essential facets in leadership today. The epic showcases various leadership styles through its characters, allowing modern leaders to draw parallels to contemporary business scenarios. For instance, Yudhishthira embodies integrity and principled leadership, while Bhima represents strength and loyalty, and Karna signifies warrior-like determination, presenting a spectrum of leadership qualities that can be emulated in business settings. The epic also provides invaluable insights into conflict resolution, as the Kurukshetra war serves as a metaphor for the conflicts faced by organizations. The multitude of strategies employed during the war highlights the importance of negotiation, understanding opposing viewpoints, and finding common ground—skills that are indispensable in today's business environments where collaboration often leads to innovative solutions. The lessons on ethical dilemmas, as portrayed through characters that grapple with choices that affect their personal and professional lives, offer modern executives a framework for making principled decisions amidst competing interests and pressures.

The narrative underscores the significance of adaptability and strategic planning. Just as the characters had to adapt their strategies based on the evolving circumstances of the war, businesses today must remain agile, continually reassessing market dynamics and adjusting their strategies accordingly. The Mahabharata also emphasizes the unavoidable nature of competition, illustrating that businesses must navigate rivalries and market challenges with resilience and foresight.

Furthermore, the Mahabharata's account of diverse characters, ranging from the virtuous to the flawed, reflects the diverse human nature observed in modern workplaces. Understanding these character nuances assists leaders and managers in fostering inclusive environments that value individual strengths while addressing weaknesses constructively. The relevance of the Mahabharata to modern business extends into numerous domains, including ethics, leadership, conflict management, and strategy, making it a timeless resource for professionals seeking guidance on navigating the complexities of the current business landscape. By embracing the wisdom embedded in this ancient text, modern business leaders can cultivate organizations that not only strive for success but do so with integrity, accountability, and respect for all stakeholders involved, thereby reinforcing the notion that true success lies in harmonizing profit motives with societal well-being.

Introduction to the concept of Corporate Mahabharata

The concept of Corporate Mahabharata arises from the ancient Indian epic, the Mahabharata, which serves as a rich narrative replete with moral complexities, ethical dilemmas, and strategic interactions among its characters that closely parallel the challenges faced in contemporary corporate environments. At its core, the Corporate Mahabharata framework emphasizes the understanding of business as a multifaceted arena where ethical considerations, power dynamics, and human relationships play critical roles in determining outcomes, much like the epic's portrayal of the Kurukshetra war. In business, as in the Mahabharata, conflicts often arise not merely from competition for resources, but from differing values, loyalties, and interpretations of duty (dharma). This concept encourages organizations to engage with moral frameworks that prioritize not just profitability but also social responsibility, ethical governance, and holistic stakeholder engagement. The Mahabharata exemplifies the importance of dharma—an individual's duty and moral obligation—which resonates with modern discussions surrounding corporate social responsibility (CSR), and the need for businesses to navigate their operations harmoniously with ethical principles and community welfare. The depiction of leaders in the Mahabharata, such as Yudhishthira, who embodies integrity and fairness, serves as a model for contemporary business leaders who are increasingly called to lead with transparency and ethics in mind, steering their organizations through the complexities of market dynamics while holding true to their values. By reflecting on the trials faced by characters such as Arjuna, who confronts moral paralysis in the face of duty, corporate leaders can better understand the necessity of making tough decisions that balance financial imperatives with ethical considerations, thus fostering a culture of principled decision-making in their organizations. Furthermore, the various interpersonal relationships depicted in the Mahabharata—betrayals, loyalty, rivalry—are mirrored in the corporate world, where interpersonal dynamics significantly influence organizational culture and employee engagement. The alliances and conflicts among the Pandavas and Kauravas highlight the relevance of strategic relationships and the impacts of trust and betrayal in business partnerships. In essence, the Corporate Mahabharata serves as a cautionary tale, urging leaders to cultivate environments of trust, open communication, and mutual respect. The battlefield of Kurukshetra serves as a metaphor for the competitive business landscape, wherein organizations must strategize, adapt, and respond to both internal and external pressures, recognizing that the path to success is often fraught with moral ambiguity.

The concept of Corporate Mahabharata also draws upon lessons from the epic regarding conflict resolution and negotiation, showcasing various strategies employed by characters to resolve disputes and achieve their objectives. For example, Krishna's role as a mediator embodies the significance of diplomacy and negotiation in addressing conflicts, which businesses can employ to resolve disputes amicably rather than resorting to adversarial tactics. The lessons of inclusivity and respect for diversity present within the Mahabharata narrative can also guide organizations in fostering a corporate culture that values diverse perspectives, encouraging innovation and collaboration in problem-solving while recognizing and addressing biases that may hinder progress.

Moreover, the Corporate Mahabharata concept prompts businesses to reflect on their narratives, values, and missions. Just as the Mahabharata is a story that encompasses various characters, conflicts, and resolutions, so too can a corporation's story be shaped by its history, challenges, and triumphs. This narrative approach allows companies to engage more deeply with their stakeholders, creating a sense of identity and purpose that transcends mere economic transactions. In today's context, where stakeholders demand greater accountability and transparency, integrating lessons from the Mahabharata into corporate strategy can serve as an effective approach to developing a brand that resonates with consumers who are increasingly aligned with values-driven enterprises.

The Corporate Mahabharata concept provides invaluable insights for navigating the complexities of modern business. By emphasizing ethical decision-making, building trust within relationships and crafting a compelling corporate narrative, organizations can learn to balance their ambitions with their responsibilities. This alignment of purpose not only contributes to the long-term sustainability of the business but also enhances its reputation and trustworthiness in the marketplace, ultimately leading to a more equitable and just business environment. Harnessing the wisdom of the Mahabharata within a corporate framework can pave the way for leaders to navigate their enterprises through ethical and moral landscapes, ensuring that they not only seek profit but also contribute meaningfully to society at large, thus reflecting the deeper values inherent in both the epic and modern corporate strategies.

How ancient wisdom can apply to contemporary corporate ethics and strategies

Exploring the relevance of ancient wisdom to contemporary corporate ethics and strategies reveals a rich tapestry of insights that can guide modern businesses through the complexities of today's globalized economy. Ancient philosophies such as those derived from Confucianism, Stoicism, and various Eastern traditions emphasize ethical behavior, the importance of community and relationships, and the moral dimensions of decision-making, all of which are crucial in fostering sustainable business practices. For instance, the teachings of Confucius promote the values of Ren (compassion), Li (propriety), and Yi (righteousness), urging leaders to adopt a holistic approach that balances profit with social responsibility. These principles can be integrated into corporate governance frameworks, encouraging organizations to measure success not solely by financial returns but also by their contributions to societal welfare. Moreover, the lessons from ancient Greek philosophers, particularly Aristotle, underscore the concept of virtue ethics that focuses on character and integrity. In contemporary corporate environments, this translates to fostering a culture of trust and ethical behavior among employees and stakeholders, promoting a work environment where ethical considerations guide decision-making processes. The application of Aristotle's idea of the "Golden Mean," which advocates for moderation and balance in action, can help businesses create strategies that avoid extremes and emphasize long-term benefits over short-term gains.

Ancient Indian scriptures advocate for Dharma, or righteous duty, which encourages businesses to operate in accordance with ethical principles and social responsibilities. This notion profoundly aligns with modern corporate social responsibility (CSR) initiatives, wherein businesses acknowledge their obligations to all stakeholders, including employees, customers, and the community. Companies such as Tata Group exemplify this principle, demonstrating that adhering to ethical practices not only enhances corporate reputation but also leads to long-term sustainability. The holistic approaches present in ancient wisdom highlight the interdependence of individuals and organizations within their communities, promoting a collaborative mindset conducive to innovation and ethical excellence.

The Stoic philosophy offers insights into resilience and moral fortitude, emphasizing the importance of maintaining ethical standards even amid challenges. In a rapidly changing business landscape marked by ethical dilemmas and crises, the Stoic belief in self-discipline and virtue can equip leaders with the tools necessary to navigate complexities while staying true to their values. This approach can also inform the development of ethical guidelines that foster accountability and transparency, essential components in today's business ethics discussions.

In addition to these philosophical foundations, ancient wisdom encourages organizations to foster environments that prioritize wisdom and learning. The concept of "organizational wisdom," derived from various ancient traditions, emphasizes the importance of reflection, learning from past experiences, and adapting strategies based on ethical considerations. Businesses can cultivate wisdom through practices such as mindfulness and continuous education, ensuring that employees are equipped with the moral frameworks to address ethical challenges thoughtfully. Moreover, ancient texts like Sun Tzu's "The Art of War" provide strategic insights that transcend mere conflict management to include ethical leadership and decision-making. The principles of strategic thinking, adaptability, and the importance of understanding one's environment are applicable in corporate strategies aimed at achieving sustainable competitive advantage. By embracing these strategic insights alongside ethical considerations, companies can formulate comprehensive strategies that not only focus on profitability but also prioritize ethical imperatives and societal impact. The application of ancient wisdom to contemporary corporate ethics and strategies lays a foundational framework that empowers modern organizations to address ethical dilemmas proactively while fostering sustainable practices. By integrating insights from various ancient philosophies, businesses can cultivate a culture of integrity, resilience, and social responsibility, ultimately contributing to a more equitable and sustainable global economy. This synthesis of ancient teachings into the fabric of modern corporate ethics not only honors the wisdom of the past but also paves the way for future generations of leaders and organizations committed to ethical excellence and the betterment of society. Embracing these ancient perspectives can lead to a profound transformation in how businesses operate, making them not just profit-driven entities but responsible stewards of societal and ethical values, ensuring their relevance and sustainability in an ever-evolving marketplace

Acknowledgements

I would like to express my heartfelt gratitude to my beloved family, whose unwavering support and encouragement have been the foundation of my journey. Your belief in my vision has fueled my passion for this work. I am also deeply thankful to the Institute of Engineering & Management, Kolkata, for nurturing my intellect and providing the tools necessary to explore the connections between corporate strategy and ancient wisdom. Your guidance has been invaluable. Lastly, I acknowledge the Almighty for illuminating my path and granting me the strength to pursue this endeavor. May this work reflect the timeless teachings of the Mahabharata, inspiring future leaders in ethical governance.

❦

CHAPTER ONE

Corporate Conflict & Competition

The Battle of Kurukshetra - Corporate Conflict and Competition

The Battle of Kurukshetra, as depicted in the Indian epic Mahabharata, serves as a profound allegory for corporate conflict and competition, illustrating the complex moral dilemmas, power struggles, and ethical considerations that arise in business environments today. In this epic, the righteous Pandavas and the ambitious Kauravas engage in a fierce struggle for power, reflecting how corporate entities often contend for market dominance, resources, and strategic advantages. At the core of this conflict lies the concept of Dharma, or righteousness, which parallels the ethical responsibilities companies have toward their stakeholders, including employees, customers, and society at large. The Kurukshetra battlefield is symbolic of the corporate arena, where decisions are often marked by high stakes, competitive maneuvering, and conflicting interests. Just as the Pandavas faced dilemmas about duty and morality in combat, such as Arjuna's initial reluctance to wage war against his kin, corporate leaders frequently confront ethical questions about the impacts of their decisions on various stakeholders, forcing them to balance profit motives with social responsibility. The strategic alliances, betrayals, and advertisements for supremacy in the Mahabharata echo the competitive tactics employed by firms vying for market share, where collaboration and rivalry coexist, reminiscent of contemporary corporate dynamics where joint ventures and partnerships can rapidly shift to fierce competition for market positioning. The ultimate lesson of the Kurukshetra war highlights that victory in business, much like in battle, is not solely determined by power or resources, but by the adherence to ethical principles and the long-term vision for sustainability.

The moral ambiguities faced by the characters in the Mahabharata underscore the importance of corporate governance and accountability, as companies must navigate the fine line between aggressive competition and ethical conduct, ensuring that their pursuit of advantage does not come at the expense of ethical standards or stakeholder trust. The emphasis on strategic planning in the Mahabharata, particularly through characters like Krishna who served as mentor and strategist for the Pandavas, mirrors the role of corporate strategists and advisors in guiding firms through turbulent market landscapes. Competitive strategies, much like the alliances formed in the Kurukshetra, can lead to both advantageous outcomes and unforeseen consequences, necessitating forward-thinking approaches to risk management and ethical foresight. Furthermore, the themes of loyalty and betrayal, which permeate the narrative, reflect the challenges organizations face in maintaining integrity and trust amidst the cutthroat nature of business. The lessons drawn from the epic illuminate the need for corporations to cultivate ethical cultures that prioritize transparency and accountability, as these qualities are essential in fostering sustainable business practices that engender loyalty among customers and employees alike.

The Battle of Kurukshetra also serves as a cautionary tale regarding the consequences of unchecked ambition and hubris, where the Kauravas' desire for power leads to their ultimate downfall, paralleling how corporate greed can result in catastrophic failures and scandals. Organizations that prioritize short-term gains without considering their broader impact risk damaging their reputation and eroding stakeholder trust, similar to how the Kauravas lost the allegiance of their own supporters throughout the conflict. The unfolding narrative not only reveals the personal sacrifices made by the characters, embodying themes of nobility, duty, and courage, but also emphasizes the importance of aligning corporate actions with ethical standards and community values. Furthermore, the intersection of personal and corporate battles portrayed in the Mahabharata emphasizes the human element within organizations, illustrating how individual motivations, ambitions, and ethical stances can significantly shape a company's culture and operational outcomes.

In essence, the Battle of Kurukshetra serves as a powerful metaphor for corporate conflict and competition, reinforcing the idea that the outcomes of business engagements are deeply intertwined with ethical considerations and moral responsibilities. As companies navigate the complexities of the modern marketplace, the ancient wisdom encapsulated in this epic encourages business leaders to reflect on the greater implications of their decisions, fostering cultures that prioritize ethical leadership, social responsibility, and accountability. The ultimate resolution of the Mahabharata, where the triumph of good over evil is celebrated, speaks to the enduring belief that ethical conduct and virtue shall prevail in the long run, guiding organizations toward sustainable success and resonating with the growing importance of corporate social responsibility in contemporary business practices. Thus, the Battle of Kurukshetra remains not just a historical or mythological account, but a timeless narrative that continues to inform and inspire ethical considerations in the fierce arena of corporate competition, offering invaluable lessons in duty, integrity, and the strategic balance of power within the ever-evolving landscape of business.

The Nature of Corporate Rivalry

Exploring the nature of corporate rivalry through the lens of the Mahabharata reveals deep insights into competition, strategy, and ethical considerations that resonate in today's business world. The epic is not just a narrative of familial conflict but a complex exploration of rivalry, where the stakes involve power, resources, and moral dilemmas. Central to the Mahabharata is the competition between the Pandavas and Kauravas, which serves as an allegory for corporate rivalry. This conflict is driven by ambition, jealousy, and the desire for supremacy, paralleling the motivations that often fuel corporate competition. The characters embody various aspects of rivalry—Duryodhana's relentless pursuit of power and the Pandavas' struggle for rightful recognition echo the fierce competition seen in the corporate landscape. Duryodhana, akin to an ambitious corporate leader, exhibits traits of strategic cunning, seeking to undermine his rivals through manipulation and deceit, reflecting how cutthroat competition can often lead to unethical practices in business. His tactics, such as the infamous game of dice, symbolize how some corporate players resort to underhanded methods to gain an upper hand, illustrating the darker side of rivalry where ethics are compromised for victory. In contrast, Yudhishthira, representing integrity and adherence to dharma, showcases the ideal of competing with honor. His character serves as a reminder that corporate rivalry can be navigated with ethical considerations, highlighting that success achieved through integrity fosters long-term sustainability and respect in the business realm.

The Mahabharata also illustrates the importance of alliances and strategic partnerships in the context of rivalry. Just as the Pandavas formed alliances with key figures like Krishna and the Panchalas to bolster their position, businesses often engage in strategic alliances to enhance competitiveness and market presence. The dynamics of these alliances reveal the complexities of corporate relationships, where trust and shared goals can lead to greater strength against common rivals. However, the epic also serves as a cautionary tale, illustrating how alliances can shift and betrayals can occur, reminding business leaders of the precarious nature of partnerships in the competitive landscape. Additionally, the lessons of warfare in the Mahabharata, particularly the Kurukshetra battle, parallel corporate battles in the marketplace, where strategic planning, resource allocation, and execution are crucial. The preparation for war, including gathering intelligence and understanding the strengths and weaknesses of opponents, mirrors how companies conduct market research and competitive analysis to position themselves effectively against rivals. The role of Krishna as a strategist and advisor emphasizes the importance of mentorship and wise counsel in navigating corporate rivalry. His guidance to Arjuna highlights that success is not solely determined by strength but also by strategy, foresight, and ethical decision-making, a principle that can guide leaders in their approach to competition.

Moreover, the Mahabharata addresses the psychological dimensions of rivalry, particularly through characters' motivations and actions. The intense emotions—greed, envy, and pride—exhibited by Duryodhana and his followers illustrate how personal rivalries can escalate into broader conflicts. In the corporate world, these emotions can manifest in various forms, such as unhealthy competition, toxic work environments, and retaliatory actions. The consequences of such rivalries often lead to a loss of focus on core business objectives and ethical standards, resulting in damage to reputations and long-term sustainability. The tragic downfall of characters like Duryodhana serves as a stark reminder that unchecked ambition and malice can lead to self-destruction, urging modern corporate leaders to reflect on the moral implications of their competitive strategies. The narrative also emphasizes the importance of resilience and adaptability in the face of rivalry. The Pandavas, despite facing numerous challenges and setbacks, persist in their quest for justice and rightful leadership. This resilience is crucial in the corporate sphere, where companies often encounter fierce competition and must navigate changing market dynamics. Learning from failures, adapting strategies, and maintaining a long-term vision are essential traits for success, as demonstrated by the Pandavas' journey toward reclaiming their kingdom.

Furthermore, the epic highlights the significance of legacy and the long-term impacts of rivalry. The outcomes of the Mahabharata's conflicts not only determine the fate of its characters but also shape future generations. This notion of legacy resonates strongly in the corporate world, where the actions of leaders can have lasting effects on company culture, stakeholder trust, and societal impact. Businesses that prioritize ethical competition and social responsibility create a positive legacy, fostering loyalty and respect among customers and employees alike. In contrast, those who engage in unethical practices may achieve short-term gains but risk long-term repercussions that can tarnish their brand and erode trust. The Mahabharata ultimately serves as a profound exploration of the nature of rivalry, offering lessons that transcend its time and context. By examining the epic's characters, strategies, and moral dilemmas, contemporary leaders can glean insights into navigating corporate competition with integrity and foresight. The narrative encourages a holistic understanding of rivalry—not merely as a struggle for dominance but as a complex interplay of relationships, ethics, and long-term consequences. In embracing these lessons, business leaders can aspire to build competitive organizations that thrive not only in the marketplace but also in their commitment to ethical practices and social responsibility, ensuring that their legacy reflects values of honor and justice rather than mere conquest. Thus, the Mahabharata continues to be relevant in its portrayal of rivalry, providing a rich tapestry of insights that can guide individuals and organizations in navigating the multifaceted nature of competition in the corporate world.

Case studies of modern corporate conflicts

Examining modern corporate conflicts through the lens of the Mahabharata reveals striking parallels that underscore the timeless nature of rivalry, strategy, and ethical dilemmas in the business world. One of the most prominent examples of corporate conflict can be found in the battle between tech giants like Apple and Samsung, reminiscent of the epic struggle between the Pandavas and Kauravas. This rivalry, characterized by fierce competition over market share, innovation, and brand loyalty, highlights how companies can engage in a relentless pursuit of supremacy that mirrors the bitter feud between these two families in the Mahabharata. Both sides have exhibited traits similar to Duryodhana and Yudhishthira, with Apple often embodying a more principled, design-centric approach that focuses on user experience and ecosystem integration, while Samsung has leveraged its resources and aggressive marketing strategies to capture a broader market. This dynamic illustrates the various tactics employed in corporate rivalry, where innovation and ethical practices can sometimes clash with aggressive tactics and competitive maneuvers. The legal battles between these companies, involving patents and intellectual property, serve as modern equivalents to the strategic battles fought in Kurukshetra, where each side seeks to outmaneuver the other in a bid for dominance, paralleling the tactical ingenuity displayed by characters like Krishna and Arjuna during their quest for victory.

Another relevant case study is the conflict between Uber and Lyft, two ride-sharing companies that have competed fiercely for market leadership, akin to the Pandavas' struggle for their rightful place in society. This rivalry is marked by aggressive marketing campaigns, strategic partnerships, and occasional corporate espionage, echoing the underhanded tactics employed by Duryodhana against his brothers. Just as the Pandavas relied on alliances to strengthen their position, Lyft has often sought partnerships to enhance its market presence, attempting to counterbalance Uber's dominance. However, the ethical considerations surrounding both companies, particularly in terms of driver treatment, regulatory challenges, and competition practices, parallel the moral dilemmas faced by characters in the Mahabharata. The debate over who can claim the moral high ground in this rivalry invites comparisons to the conflict between Dharma and Adharma, urging modern leaders to reflect on the implications of their strategies and the ethical foundations of their business practices. The ride-sharing conflict illustrates how corporate battles are not solely about market share; they also encompass deeper issues of ethics, responsibility, and the impact of business practices on society, much like the broader themes present in the Mahabharata.

The fierce rivalry between Boeing and Airbus in the aerospace industry further exemplifies corporate conflict in a manner reminiscent of the epic's grand scale battles. The two companies, vying for dominance in the commercial aircraft market, engage in a complex interplay of competition, alliances, and geopolitical maneuvering. Similar to the alliances and betrayals depicted in the Mahabharata, Boeing and Airbus navigate a landscape where government support, international regulations, and market strategies intertwine, influencing their ability to compete effectively. The ethical implications of their rivalry came to the forefront during the Boeing 737 MAX crisis, where safety concerns and corporate practices raised questions about accountability and integrity. This situation parallels the moral complexities faced by the characters in the Mahabharata, where the consequences of one's actions can reverberate far beyond the immediate conflict. Boeing's struggle to regain public trust after the tragedy can be likened to the Pandavas' quest for justice and rightful recognition after their exile, emphasizing the importance of ethical leadership and the responsibility companies have to their stakeholders. The Boeing-Airbus rivalry illustrates how corporate conflicts are not only about competition for market share but also about the broader implications of corporate practices on society and the ethical dilemmas that arise in the pursuit of success.

In the realm of entertainment, the conflict between Netflix and traditional media companies presents another case study that resonates with themes from the Mahabharata. The rise of streaming services has disrupted traditional broadcasting, leading to intense competition as companies vie for audience attention and content supremacy. Netflix, akin to the Pandavas, has leveraged innovation and original programming to carve out a significant market position, challenging established players who are often reluctant to adapt. This struggle mirrors the conflicts between the progressive values represented by the Pandavas and the traditional values embodied by the Kauravas. The narrative surrounding this rivalry encompasses issues of content control, intellectual property, and the evolving landscape of media consumption. Traditional media companies, like the Kauravas, often rely on their established dominance and historical significance, while Netflix exemplifies the disruptive force of innovation and adaptability. The ongoing conflict raises ethical questions about the treatment of creators, the impact of monopolistic practices, and the future of content distribution, echoing the moral dilemmas faced by the characters in the Mahabharata. As companies navigate this rapidly changing environment, the lessons of adaptability, resilience, and ethical consideration are vital, highlighting the need for a balance between innovation and responsibility.

The corporate conflict between Facebook and various regulatory bodies and rival tech companies can also be contextualized within the framework of the Mahabharata. Facebook's dominant position in social media has led to significant scrutiny over data privacy, misinformation, and ethical practices, akin to the scrutiny faced by the Pandavas as they navigated their claim to legitimacy. The company's aggressive strategies for growth, including acquisitions and the expansion of its platform, reflect the ambitions of Duryodhana, who often sought to consolidate power at any cost. However, the backlash against Facebook's practices parallels the moral and ethical conflicts present in the Mahabharata, where the consequences of actions extend beyond the immediate struggle for power. Regulatory challenges and public criticism of Facebook serve as reminders that the pursuit of dominance must be tempered with responsibility and ethical considerations, much like the overarching themes of dharma and justice in the epic. The ongoing conflict highlights the need for corporate leaders to be vigilant about the ethical implications of their strategies, urging them to consider the broader impact of their actions on society.

The rivalry in the fast-food industry, exemplified by the competition between McDonald's and Burger King, echoes the themes of the Mahabharata in its representation of strategic positioning and market tactics. This conflict involves not only product offerings and marketing strategies but also broader cultural narratives surrounding food, health, and sustainability. The intense competition between these two giants is reminiscent of the interpersonal conflicts among the Kauravas and Pandavas, where each side seeks to outdo the other through various tactics, including aggressive advertising and menu innovations. The ethical considerations surrounding fast food, particularly in terms of health impacts and labor practices, parallel the moral dilemmas faced by characters in the Mahabharata. Just as the Pandavas grappled with their sense of duty and righteousness, modern corporations must navigate the balance between profit motives and social responsibility. The fast-food rivalry serves as a microcosm of broader societal issues, illustrating how corporate conflicts can reflect and shape cultural narratives and ethical considerations in a rapidly changing landscape.

The exploration of modern corporate conflicts through the lens of the Mahabharata reveals profound insights into the nature of rivalry, strategy, and ethical dilemmas in the business world. Each case study exemplifies how themes of ambition, integrity, and accountability manifest in contemporary settings, reflecting the enduring relevance of the epic's lessons. The narratives of the Pandavas and Kauravas provide a framework for understanding the complexities of corporate competition, encouraging leaders to consider not only their strategic maneuvers but also the ethical implications of their actions. As businesses continue to navigate the challenges of a dynamic marketplace, the Mahabharata offers timeless wisdom that can guide decision-making and foster a culture of responsibility, ensuring that the legacy of corporate rivalry is one of honor and ethical leadership rather than mere conquest. Ultimately, the insights gleaned from these modern conflicts remind us that the struggles we face in the corporate world are not just about winning or losing but about the values we uphold and the impact we have on society as a whole.

Lessons from the Mahabharata on Strategy

Exploring the Mahabharata for lessons on strategy reveals profound insights that extend far beyond the epic's narrative, offering valuable guidance for leaders in various fields, particularly in the realms of business and warfare. The epic's characters and their actions exemplify different strategic principles that are applicable in modern contexts, illustrating the importance of foresight, adaptability, and ethical considerations in formulating effective strategies. At the heart of the Mahabharata is the Kurukshetra war, a grand conflict that serves as a backdrop for numerous strategic maneuvers, decisions, and philosophical discourses that resonate with contemporary challenges. One of the most notable strategic lessons emerges from Krishna's role as a charioteer and advisor to Arjuna. His guidance embodies the significance of mentorship and wise counsel in navigating complex situations. In the context of corporate leadership, the value of having a trusted advisor who can provide perspective and insight is paramount. Krishna's strategic acumen is evident in his ability to assess the battlefield, anticipate opponents' moves, and devise a plan that leverages the strengths of his allies while exploiting the weaknesses of the adversary. This lesson underscores the need for leaders to cultivate relationships with mentors and advisors who can offer critical insights and help navigate challenges effectively. The Mahabharata illustrates the importance of understanding one's strengths and weaknesses in strategy formulation. The Pandavas, despite facing overwhelming odds, consistently leverage their unique attributes to gain an advantage over the Kauravas. For instance, Bhima's immense strength, Arjuna's unparalleled archery skills, and Nakula and Sahadeva's expertise in horse riding become pivotal in the conflict. This reflects the principle of strategic alignment; where recognizing and utilizing the individual strengths of team members can lead to collective success. In a corporate environment, this translates into the need for leaders to identify and harness the diverse talents within their teams, fostering a culture of collaboration that capitalizes on each member's unique contributions. Moreover, the contrasting strategies employed by the Kauravas, particularly Duryodhana's reliance on brute force and manipulation, serve as a cautionary tale about the pitfalls of underestimating opponents and neglecting ethical considerations. Duryodhana's ambition and willingness to engage in deceitful tactics ultimately lead to his downfall, reinforcing the idea that strategies rooted in integrity and respect for opponents are more sustainable in the long run.

Another vital lesson from the Mahabharata is the importance of adaptability and flexibility in strategy. The characters frequently encounter unforeseen challenges that require them to pivot their plans and reassess their approaches. For example, Arjuna's initial reluctance to engage in battle against his own kin illustrates the emotional and ethical dilemmas that can arise in strategic decision-making. Krishna's counsel encourages him to adapt his mindset and embrace his duty as a warrior, highlighting the need for leaders to remain open to change and to reassess their strategies in response to evolving circumstances. In business, this adaptability is crucial, as leaders must navigate shifting market conditions, emerging technologies, and evolving consumer preferences. The ability to pivot and innovate in response to challenges can be a decisive factor in achieving success, just as it was for the Pandavas in their quest for victory.

As, Mahabharata emphasizes the significance of information and intelligence in strategy formulation, characters like Sanjaya, who provides a real-time account of the battle to Dhritarashtra, exemplify the critical role of accurate information in decision-making. The Pandavas' strategic advantage stems from their ability to gather intelligence about their enemies and leverage that knowledge in battle. This principle resonates strongly in the modern corporate world, where data-driven decision-making and market intelligence are paramount. Leaders must prioritize gathering relevant information, analyzing market trends, and understanding competitors to formulate effective strategies that enhance their competitive edge. The Mahabharata also illustrates the value of deception and psychological strategy, as seen in the use of the "Maya" or illusion in warfare. The construction of the illusory palace of Lakshagriha and the subsequent attempt to trap the Pandavas underscores the idea that perception can be as powerful as reality in shaping outcomes. This lesson is relevant in competitive scenarios, where creating a strong brand presence and managing public perception can significantly impact market positioning. The role of alliances and relationships in strategy is another crucial theme explored in the Mahabharata. The Pandavas' success is, in part, attributed to their ability to forge alliances with key figures such as Krishna and the Panchalas. This reflects the importance of collaboration and coalition-building in achieving strategic objectives. In contemporary contexts, forming strategic partnerships and alliances can enhance capabilities, expand market reach, and create synergies that benefit all parties involved. Leaders who understand the power of collaboration and prioritize building strong relationships are better positioned to navigate complex challenges and achieve long-term success. The epic also highlights the moral complexities inherent in strategy. Characters often grapple with ethical dilemmas, such as Arjuna's conflict over fighting against his kin. Krishna's guidance emphasizes that while strategic success is important, it must be pursued within the framework of dharma (righteousness). This underscores the critical need for leaders to align their strategies with ethical principles and societal values, recognizing that sustainable success is rooted in integrity and accountability.

The Mahabharata also illustrates the impact of timing in strategic decision-making. The pivotal moments in the epic, such as Krishna's divine revelation to Arjuna at the onset of battle, emphasize the importance of seizing opportunities at the right moment. Leaders must be attuned to market dynamics and poised to act decisively when opportunities arise. This lesson on timing is particularly relevant in fast-paced industries where delays in decision-making can result in missed opportunities and loss of competitive advantage. The notion of sacrifice and the greater good also permeates the strategic lessons of the Mahabharata. Characters like Arjuna are faced with choices that involve personal sacrifice for the greater benefit of society. This theme resonates strongly in contemporary leadership, where decisions often require weighing individual interests against the collective good. Leaders who prioritize the welfare of their teams and stakeholders, even at personal or organizational cost, cultivate trust and loyalty, reinforcing their strategic position in the long term. Ancient text provides insights into the significance of resilience and perseverance in strategy. The Pandavas endure numerous trials and tribulations, from their exile to the eventual battle, demonstrating that success is not merely about winning but also about the ability to withstand challenges and maintain focus on long-term goals. This resilience is crucial for leaders in today's volatile business environment, where setbacks and failures are inevitable. The ability to learn from adversity, adapt strategies, and persist in the face of obstacles can differentiate successful organizations from those that falter. Additionally, the Mahabharata underscores the value of ethical leadership and the responsibility of those in power. The characters are frequently faced with choices that test their integrity, and their decisions have far-reaching consequences for themselves and their communities. This highlights the importance of cultivating a leadership style that prioritizes ethical considerations and the welfare of stakeholders. Leaders who embody ethical principles not only foster a positive organizational culture but also enhance their reputation and build long-lasting relationships with customers and partners.

As the Mahabharata unfolds, the theme of legacy becomes increasingly prominent, reminding leaders that the strategies they employ today will shape the narratives of the future. Just as the outcomes of the Kurukshetra war determined the fate of the characters and their families, the decisions made in the corporate world can have lasting impacts on future generations. Leaders must be mindful of the legacies they create, ensuring that their strategies contribute positively to society and reflect values of justice, fairness, and respect for all stakeholders. In conclusion, the Mahabharata offers a rich tapestry of strategic lessons that are as relevant today as they were in ancient times. The epic's exploration of mentorship, adaptability, intelligence, collaboration, and ethical considerations provides a comprehensive framework for understanding the complexities of strategy. By drawing from the wisdom embedded in the Mahabharata, contemporary leaders can navigate the challenges of their respective fields with foresight, integrity, and a commitment to the greater good. The insights gleaned from this ancient text remind us that strategy is not merely a tool for competition but a reflection of values, relationships, and the legacy we leave behind. Ultimately, the lessons of the Mahabharata empower leaders to approach strategy with a holistic perspective that encompasses both the tactical and ethical dimensions of their endeavors, fostering sustainable success and positive impact in an ever-evolving world.

Insights drawn from the tactics in the epic

The Mahabharata, an epic narrative of immense scope and depth, offers rich insights into human nature, ethics, and the complexities of leadership through its multifaceted characters and their strategic approaches. Each character embodies specific tactics and strategies, providing timeless lessons that resonate across cultures and eras. Central to the narrative is the great Kurukshetra War, a conflict that transcends mere territorial ambition, exploring themes of duty (dharma), righteousness, and moral conflict. This examination delves into the diverse strategies employed by characters such as Arjuna, Krishna, Duryodhana, Bhishma, Karna, and Draupadi, revealing profound insights into the nature of conflict, leadership, and ethical dilemmas.

Arjuna

Arjuna serves as one of the most compelling figures in the Mahabharata, grappling with profound moral dilemmas that resonate with the human experience. His journey begins with a crisis of conscience as he stands on the battlefield, facing the prospect of fighting against his own relatives. Arjuna's initial refusal to engage in battle highlights a critical insight: the tension between personal ethics and societal duties. This internal struggle is resolved through his dialogue with Krishna, who imparts spiritual wisdom and guidance. Arjuna's eventual acceptance of his duty as a warrior underscores the importance of reconciling personal beliefs with responsibilities. His journey teaches us that in moments of ethical uncertainty, seeking guidance and clarity can illuminate the path forward, a strategy applicable to both personal and professional dilemmas.

Lord Krishna

Krishna, the divine charioteer and strategist, embodies a multifaceted approach to leadership and conflict resolution. His role in the epic is pivotal, not only as Arjuna's guide but also as a master tactician who navigates the complexities of diplomacy, manipulation, and wisdom. Krishna's attempts at negotiation prior to the war reflect a fundamental tactic: the importance of dialogue and peaceful resolution. When diplomacy fails, his strategic interventions during the war, such as the psychological tactics used to instill fear and confusion among the Kauravas, emphasize the need for adaptability in leadership. Krishna's wisdom teaches that effective strategies often require a blend of direct action and subtle manipulation, reminding us that not all challenges can be confronted head-on. His actions illustrate that the most successful leaders must be versatile, employing a range of tactics to achieve their goals while remaining committed to a righteous cause.

Duryodhana

In stark contrast to Krishna's wisdom, Duryodhana, the Kaurava prince, exemplifies the darker aspects of ambition and leadership. His relentless pursuit of power and his willingness to engage in deceitful tactics serve as cautionary tales about the consequences of unethical behavior. Duryodhana's strategies often involve manipulation and betrayal, showcasing a singular focus on victory at any cost. His failure to recognize the value of loyalty and ethical conduct ultimately leads to his downfall. The lessons drawn from Duryodhana's character highlight the perils of ambition divorced from morality. His story illustrates that while determination and strategy are vital for success, the means by which one seeks power can significantly affect outcomes, both personally and for society at large. This character serves as a reminder that unethical strategies can lead not only to individual ruin but also to widespread suffering, reinforcing the idea that true leadership requires a foundation of integrity.

Bhishma

Bhishma, the revered patriarch of the Kuru dynasty, embodies loyalty, sacrifice, and the complexities of duty. His life is marked by a vow of celibacy and a commitment to the throne, often leading him to make painful choices for the greater good. Bhishma's strategies reflect a deep understanding of dharma, as he navigates his loyalties to both the Kauravas and Pandavas. His decision to fight for the Kauravas, despite his affection for the Pandavas, illustrates the difficult choices leaders must make when their duties conflict with personal feelings. Bhishma's character teaches that true leadership often requires personal sacrifice and an unwavering commitment to one's principles, even when those principles lead to hardship. His eventual defeat on the battlefield serves as a poignant reminder of the transient nature of power and the importance of aligning one's actions with ethical beliefs.

Karna

Karna, another tragic figure, offers a different perspective on loyalty and identity. Born to Kunti and the sun god but raised as a charioteer's son, Karna's life is defined by his quest for respect and recognition. His unwavering loyalty to Duryodhana, despite the moral compromises it entails, highlights the complexities of friendship and honor. Karna's strategies are influenced by his desire to prove him, often leading him to make choices that conflict with his inherent sense of right and wrong. His tragic end underscores the consequences of misplaced loyalty and the struggle between societal identity and personal values. Karna's character invites reflection on the nature of fate versus free will, illustrating how one's background and choices can shape destiny. His life serves as a reminder of the importance of understanding one's values and making choices that align with one's true self, rather than succumbing to external pressures.

Draupadi

The role of Draupadi, the epic's central female character, further enriches the narrative with themes of resilience and agency. Her fierce determination and strategic acumen come to the forefront during the infamous dice game, where she challenges the Kauravas' dishonor. Draupadi's ability to assert herself in a patriarchal society underscores the importance of standing up for one's dignity and rights. Her character exemplifies the idea that strength is not merely physical but can manifest through courage and strategic thinking. Draupadi's narrative teaches that female agency is a powerful force in any struggle for justice. She becomes a catalyst for the conflict, illustrating how individual actions can influence broader societal events. Her resilience amid adversity serves as an inspiration for those facing challenges, reinforcing the importance of using one's voice and standing firm in the pursuit of justice.

In addition to the individual strategies, the Mahabharata also highlights the significance of alliances and loyalty. The relationships between characters often dictate the course of events, emphasizing that collaboration can enhance one's strategic position. The alliance between the Pandavas and Krishna exemplifies the power of teamwork and mutual support. Krishna's strategic role as an ally demonstrates that true strength lies in collaboration, especially when navigating complex conflicts. This aspect of the narrative reflects a critical insight: the value of building and maintaining alliances, whether in personal relationships or professional settings. In a world often characterized by competition, the Mahabharata reminds us that unity and cooperation can lead to greater success and fulfillment.The broader implications of conflict and its consequences are vividly depicted in the aftermath of the Kurukshetra War. The epic delves into the toll of violence on individuals and society, painting a grim picture of the devastation wrought by war. The reflections of the surviving characters on loss and the futility of violence serve as poignant reminders of the need for reconciliation and healing in the wake of conflict. The destruction of families and the disillusionment of the victorious Pandavas underscore the idea that victory can come at an unbearable cost. This narrative arc invites readers to consider the long-term consequences of conflict and the importance of pursuing peace and understanding in a fractured world.

Yudhishthira

The Mahabharata explores the nuances of governance and ethical leadership through the character of Yudhishthira, the eldest Pandava. Yudhishthira's commitment to truth and justice, even in the face of overwhelming challenges, serves as a guiding principle for effective leadership. His decisions throughout the epic emphasize the importance of ethical considerations in governance. Yudhishthira's character highlights the idea that true leadership requires balancing personal integrity with the needs of the people. His struggles with decisions that weigh moral righteousness against pragmatic concerns illustrate the complexities inherent in leadership. The insights drawn from Yudhishthira's journey reinforce the notion that ethical leadership is not only about making difficult choices but also about fostering trust and accountability within society.

The character dynamics in the Mahabharata further illuminate the themes of conflict and resolution. The interplay between various characters, their motivations, and their strategies creates a rich tapestry of human experience. The shifting allegiances, betrayals, and reconciliations throughout the narrative highlight the fluidity of relationships and the impact they have on the unfolding drama. The epic underscores that relationships often serve as the bedrock of both conflict and resolution, illustrating that understanding the motivations and emotions of others is key to navigating complex situations.

Ultimately, the Mahabharata serves as a profound exploration of the human condition, offering insights that extend far beyond the battlefield. The tactics and strategies employed by its characters resonate with contemporary issues of ethics, leadership, and personal growth. The lessons drawn from figures like Arjuna, Krishna, Duryodhana, Bhishma, Karna, and Draupadi encourage reflection on the choices individuals make and the impact of those choices on themselves and others. In a world filled with challenges and moral ambiguities, the wisdom embedded in the Mahabharata provides a valuable framework for understanding the intricacies of human behavior and the importance of aligning one's actions with a sense of purpose and ethical responsibility.

As the Mahabharata stands as a monumental work that transcends its historical and cultural context, it offers timeless insights into the complexities of conflict, leadership, and morality. The diverse strategies and tactics employed by its characters serve as a guide for navigating the ethical dilemmas of modern life. Through its exploration of duty, righteousness, and the human condition, the Mahabharata continues to resonate with audiences today, affirming the enduring relevance of its teachings. The epic invites readers to reflect on their values, relationships, and the choices they make, reminding us that the paths we choose can profoundly shape our destinies and the world around us.

CHAPTER TWO

Ethics in Business

Dharma - Ethics in Business: Insights from the Mahabharata

The Mahabharata, one of the most revered texts in Indian literature and philosophy, provides profound insights into the concept of Dharma, which translates to duty, righteousness, and moral law. While traditionally associated with the realms of personal conduct and societal obligations, Dharma is equally applicable to the realm of business ethics. The ethical dilemmas faced by its characters offer a framework for understanding the complexities of moral decision-making in a business context. In a world where the pursuit of profit often overshadows ethical considerations, the lessons from the Mahabharata serve as a compelling reminder of the importance of aligning business practices with ethical principles.

At its core, Dharma emphasizes the importance of aligning one's actions with universal moral values, societal expectations, and personal integrity. This principle is vividly illustrated through the actions and decisions of key characters in the Mahabharata. For instance, Arjuna's moral crisis on the battlefield reflects the challenges faced by business leaders today. He grapples with the conflicting duties of a warrior and the personal relationships he holds dear, mirroring the dilemmas faced by business executives when making decisions that impact their employees, stakeholders, and communities. Arjuna's eventual acceptance of his duty, guided by Krishna's wisdom, underscores the necessity of making decisions that are not only beneficial to one but also uphold the greater good of society.

Krishna, as Arjuna's charioteer and guide, represents the embodiment of Dharma, using his divine wisdom to navigate the complexities of ethical dilemmas. His counsel to Arjuna emphasizes the importance of action aligned with righteousness, a critical lesson for business leaders who often face situations where personal gain conflicts with ethical considerations. Krishna's teachings reflect the necessity of ethical decision-making in business, advocating that leaders must consider the broader implications of their actions and strive for outcomes that foster justice and harmony. The strategies he employs to influence the course of events during the Kurukshetra War can be likened to ethical leadership in business, where guiding teams towards a common, righteous goal is paramount.

In stark contrast, Duryodhana, the Kaurava prince, embodies the darker side of ambition and unethical behavior. His relentless pursuit of power through deceit and manipulation serves as a cautionary tale for business leaders who may be tempted to prioritize short-term gains over ethical considerations. Duryodhana's tactics highlight the risks associated with unethical practices in business, such as exploitation, dishonesty, and betrayal. His ultimate downfall illustrates the long-term consequences of prioritizing personal ambition over ethical standards, reinforcing the idea that sustainable success must be built on a foundation of integrity and accountability. The Mahabharata thus offers a compelling narrative that emphasizes that unethical behavior, while sometimes yielding immediate rewards, inevitably leads to long-term repercussions that can tarnish reputations and damage relationships.

Bhishma, the wise patriarch of the Kuru dynasty, further enriches the discourse on Dharma and ethics in business. His life is characterized by profound loyalty and adherence to duty, yet he is faced with situations where his principles are tested. Bhishma's unwavering commitment to his vow of celibacy and his role in the battle, despite the personal conflict it causes, exemplifies the challenges of balancing personal values with professional responsibilities. In a business context, leaders often find themselves in positions where they must make difficult choices that align with their ethical beliefs while also fulfilling their responsibilities to stakeholders. Bhishma's character teaches that ethical leadership requires a delicate balance between personal integrity and professional obligations, urging business leaders to reflect on their values and the impact of their decisions on others.

Karna, another pivotal figure in the Mahabharata, embodies the complexities of loyalty and identity. His story illustrates the challenges of navigating personal ethics in a competitive environment. Born to Kunti yet raised as a charioteer's son, Karna faces societal prejudice throughout his life. His unwavering loyalty to Duryodhana, despite the ethical implications, raises important questions about the nature of loyalty in business. Karna's determination to prove himself and gain respect parallels the ambitions of many business leaders who strive for recognition and success. However, his tragic end serves as a poignant reminder of the consequences of loyalty when it conflicts with ethical principles. In business, blind loyalty can lead to ethical compromises, and Karna's narrative urges leaders to evaluate their allegiances critically, ensuring that their loyalty aligns with ethical conduct.

Draupadi, the strong and resilient female protagonist, adds another layer to the discourse on Dharma in business ethics. Her character illustrates the importance of standing up for one's rights and the necessity of addressing injustices, a principle that resonates with modern business practices advocating for equity and fairness. Draupadi's courage in challenging the Kauravas during the dice game reflects the need for leaders to advocate for ethical practices and to confront unethical behavior within their organizations. Her refusal to remain silent in the face of humiliation serves as a powerful reminder that ethical leadership involves not only upholding one's principles but also fostering a culture of accountability and justice within the workplace.

The dynamics of power and relationships depicted in the Mahabharata further enrich the understanding of Dharma as it pertains to business ethics. The intricate relationships among the characters reveal that business decisions are rarely made in isolation; they are influenced by the dynamics of power, loyalty, and relationships. The alliances and rivalries among the Pandavas and Kauravas exemplify how personal relationships can impact professional decisions. In business, cultivating positive relationships with stakeholders is essential for ethical conduct and long-term success. The Mahabharata teaches that fostering trust and open communication can create an environment where ethical practices thrive.

Moreover, the concept of Dharma encompasses not just individual ethics but also social responsibility. The Mahabharata emphasizes the importance of community and the collective good, urging leaders to consider the broader implications of their decisions. In modern business, corporate social responsibility (CSR) has become a critical aspect of ethical conduct, where organizations are expected to contribute positively to society. The lessons from the Mahabharata remind us that businesses have a moral obligation to consider the impact of their actions on the environment, society, and future generations. Leaders must recognize that their decisions can have far-reaching consequences and should strive to create value that benefits not only their organizations but also the communities they serve.

The epic also highlights the necessity of self-reflection and introspection in ethical decision-making. Characters like Yudhishthira, the eldest Pandava, exemplify the importance of self-awareness and moral integrity. His commitment to truth and justice, even when faced with difficult choices, underscores the role of personal values in shaping ethical behavior. Business leaders can draw from Yudhishthira's example by cultivating a culture of reflection within their organizations, encouraging team members to consider the ethical implications of their decisions and to act in accordance with their values. This introspective approach can lead to more thoughtful and responsible decision-making.

Furthermore, the Mahabharata addresses the complexities of justice and fairness, pivotal concepts in business ethics. The narrative raises critical questions about the nature of justice, particularly in the context of the Kurukshetra War. The conflict illustrates that justice is often subjective and influenced by perspectives and relationships. In business, leaders must navigate the complexities of fairness in decision-making, balancing the interests of various stakeholders while remaining committed to ethical principles. The lessons from the Mahabharata encourage leaders to adopt a holistic approach to justice, recognizing that ethical decisions must account for the diverse needs and rights of all involved.

The Mahabharata also emphasizes the significance of wisdom and discernment in ethical decision-making. Characters like Krishna embody the qualities of a wise leader, utilizing strategic thinking and foresight to guide others towards righteous actions. In a business context, leaders are often faced with complex decisions that require careful consideration of potential outcomes. The teachings of Krishna remind leaders to cultivate discernment, weighing the consequences of their actions and striving to align their decisions with ethical principles. This wisdom can help navigate the challenges of the business world, fostering a culture of integrity and accountability.

Additionally, the theme of redemption and personal growth in the Mahabharata offers valuable insights into the nature of ethical leadership. Characters like Karna and Duryodhana, despite their moral failings, are portrayed with depth and complexity, inviting reflection on the potential for change and growth. This aspect underscores the idea that ethical leadership is not solely about past actions but also about the willingness to learn, adapt, and strive for improvement. Business leaders should recognize that ethical lapses can occur and that the path to redemption involves acknowledging mistakes, taking responsibility, and committing to ethical practices moving forward. This perspective fosters a culture of continuous improvement, where individuals are encouraged to learn from their experiences and strive for ethical excellence.

The Mahabharata serves as a timeless guide to understanding Dharma and its implications for ethics in business. The characters' struggles with duty, loyalty, and moral decision-making provide a rich tapestry of lessons that are highly relevant to contemporary business practices. The insights drawn from the epic emphasize the importance of aligning business decisions with ethical principles, fostering a culture of integrity, and recognizing the broader societal impact of one's actions. As business leaders navigate the complexities of modern commerce, the teachings of the Mahabharata can serve as a powerful reminder of the enduring significance of Dharma in shaping ethical behaviour and promoting a just and equitable society. By embracing these principles, businesses can not only achieve sustainable success but also contribute positively to the world, embodying the essence of Dharma in every aspect of their operations.

Understanding Dharma in the Mahabharata

Understanding Dharma in the Mahabharata involves delving into the intricate tapestry of moral and ethical dilemmas faced by its characters, where Dharma—often translated as duty, righteousness, and law—serves as both a guiding principle and a source of profound conflict. The epic unfolds against the backdrop of the war between the Pandavas and Kauravas, and at the heart of this conflict lies Arjuna's moral crisis on the battlefield of Kurukshetra, where he grapples with the gravity of fighting against his own kin. This pivotal moment encapsulates the essence of Dharma: the struggle to balance personal emotions with societal obligations. Krishna, as Arjuna's charioteer, illuminates the complexities of Dharma through his teachings, emphasizing the importance of selfless action (karma yoga) and the necessity of adhering to one's duty regardless of personal attachments. The multifaceted nature of Dharma is further illustrated through the diverse cast of characters, each representing different facets of ethical decision-making. For instance, Yudhishthira embodies the ideals of truth and justice, often facing dilemmas that test his unwavering commitment to righteousness, while Duryodhana's relentless pursuit of power and status reveals the darker side of ambition, highlighting the consequences of deviating from ethical principles. Bhishma, the wise patriarch, grapples with his own vows and loyalties, illustrating the sacrifices inherent in the pursuit of duty, while Draupadi stands as a powerful figure advocating for justice in a patriarchal society, challenging the norms that dictate her fate. Karna's story adds another layer, as he navigates issues of identity and loyalty, struggling between his commitments to friendship and his own moral compass. The narrative does not shy away from exploring the theme of justice, depicting it as subjective and influenced by personal perspectives, a reflection on the complexities of righteousness in real life. The Mahabharata also emphasizes the interconnectedness of individual actions with the greater cosmic order, suggesting that Dharma is not merely a set of rules but a dynamic force that shapes societal well-being. Through moments of self-reflection and moral introspection, characters like Yudhishthira and Arjuna are prompted to evaluate their choices in light of their responsibilities to others. The epic ultimately presents Dharma as a living, breathing concept, challenging readers to engage with its complexities and apply its lessons to their own lives, especially in navigating the moral ambiguities of the modern world. In doing so, the Mahabharata offers a profound commentary on the nature of ethics, justice, and the human condition, inviting individuals to seek a deeper understanding of their own duties and responsibilities within the broader tapestry of society.

The concept of righteousness and duty

The concept of righteousness and duty, or Dharma, in the Mahabharata serves as the epic's foundational principle, intricately woven into the fabric of its narrative and character motivations, presenting a profound exploration of moral philosophy in the context of ancient Indian society. Dharma encompasses a wide array of meanings, from individual duties based on one's social roles and responsibilities to the broader notions of justice and ethical conduct in personal and societal spheres. Central to this discourse is Arjuna's moral dilemma on the battlefield of Kurukshetra, where he confronts the anguish of fighting against his own kin, teachers, and friends, prompting deep questions about loyalty, honor, and the ethical implications of warfare. Krishna, his charioteer, emerges as a divine guide, elucidating the nuances of Dharma by emphasizing that true righteousness often demands selflessness and adherence to one's prescribed duty, even at the cost of personal grief. This dialogue becomes a philosophical cornerstone of the epic, illustrating how individuals must often navigate the complexities of their obligations in a world rife with conflicting loyalties. The characters of the Mahabharata each embody different dimensions of righteousness and duty; for instance, Yudhishthira, the embodiment of truth and moral integrity, grapples with the demands of kingship, often placing his ethical convictions above strategic advantage, while Duryodhana, motivated by ambition and a sense of entitlement, exemplifies the perils of deviating from righteous conduct in pursuit of power. Bhishma's unwavering commitment to his vows, even as it leads to personal turmoil, illustrates the intricate relationship between duty and personal sacrifice, while Draupadi's fierce advocacy for justice in the face of humiliation highlights the moral imperative of standing against injustice, challenging the patriarchal norms that constrain her. Karna's narrative further complicates the discourse on duty; his loyalty to Duryodhana is juxtaposed with his innate sense of honor, embodying the tension between friendship and ethical principles, which ultimately leads to tragic outcomes. Throughout the epic, righteousness is portrayed not as an absolute, but as a contextual and often subjective notion, shaped by relationships, societal expectations, and personal integrity. This dynamic interplay underscores the Mahabharata's central message: that ethical decision-making is a complex journey requiring self-reflection and the courage to act in accordance with one's principles, even in the face of dire consequences. The epic invites readers to ponder the nature of justice, urging them to recognize that righteousness must also consider the welfare of the community and the cosmic order, positioning Dharma as both a personal code of conduct and a universal law governing societal harmony. Moreover, the Mahabharata suggests that true righteousness is achieved through the recognition of interconnectedness, as individual actions ripple through the social fabric, impacting others in profound ways. The characters' struggles with their respective Dharmas illustrate the idea that fulfilling one's duty can sometimes lead to moral ambiguity, challenging the notion of clear-cut righteousness and prompting deeper inquiries into the nature of good and evil. In this light, the Mahabharata serves as a timeless commentary on the ethical dilemmas faced by humanity, encouraging individuals to embrace complexity and strive for a nuanced understanding of their duties in an ever-changing world. Through its rich narrative and diverse characters, the Mahabharata ultimately posits that the journey of understanding righteousness and duty is a lifelong endeavor, one that requires wisdom, compassion, and a steadfast commitment to ethical principles in the pursuit of justice and harmony in society.

Corporate Ethics

Corporate ethics, as a concept, resonates deeply with the moral and ethical dilemmas portrayed in the Mahabharata, an ancient Indian epic that navigates complex human relationships, duty, and righteousness, thus providing valuable insights into the ethical frameworks applicable in modern business contexts. In the Mahabharata, characters are often faced with challenging decisions that reflect the principles of Dharma, or duty, which parallel the ethical responsibilities that businesses must uphold today. For instance, the battle between the Pandavas and Kauravas not only symbolizes a conflict of power and ambition but also embodies the ethical implications of leadership, where the actions of individuals impact a broader community. Yudhishthira, the eldest Pandava, represents integrity and accountability, often grappling with decisions that prioritize truth over personal gain, mirroring the ethical dilemmas corporate leaders face in balancing profit motives with moral responsibilities. His commitment to righteousness, even in the face of overwhelming odds, underscores the importance of transparency and ethical conduct in business operations. Conversely, Duryodhana's unscrupulous tactics to secure power and wealth serve as a cautionary tale about the consequences of unethical behavior, emphasizing that short-term gains achieved through deceit and manipulation can lead to long-term repercussions, including loss of reputation and trust. The epic also highlights the role of advisors and mentors in shaping ethical decisions; Krishna, as Arjuna's guide, illustrates the necessity of wise counsel in navigating complex moral landscapes, a principle that resonates with the role of ethics officers and corporate governance structures in modern organizations. Moreover, the character of Draupadi brings attention to the importance of fairness and justice in corporate ethics, as her plight during the infamous dice game signifies the need for organizations to foster a culture of respect and equity, particularly in addressing issues of gender and power dynamics within the workplace. The Mahabharata also prompts reflection on corporate social responsibility (CSR), emphasizing that the pursuit of profit must be balanced with the welfare of society and the environment, much like how characters navigate their personal duties while considering their impact on the greater community. This theme resonates in today's corporate landscape, where stakeholders increasingly demand ethical practices and accountability from businesses. Additionally, the tension between personal ambition and collective well-being is vividly illustrated through the struggles of characters like Karna, whose loyalty and ethical dilemmas reflect the challenges faced by individuals in corporate settings who must navigate their loyalties to both personal interests and organizational goals. The complexities of justice and fairness, central to the Mahabharata, challenge businesses to establish ethical frameworks that uphold justice for all stakeholders, including employees, customers, and the community at large. In essence, the Mahabharata serves as a timeless guide for corporate ethics, encouraging leaders to cultivate a moral compass that navigates the intricacies of duty, justice, and integrity in a rapidly evolving business environment, ultimately advocating for a holistic approach that prioritizes ethical considerations in the pursuit of success. By embracing the lessons embedded in the epic, contemporary organizations can foster ethical cultures that not only enhance their reputations but also contribute positively to the societal fabric, ensuring that their legacies are defined not just by financial performance, but by their commitment to ethical principles and the greater good.

How businesses can align their goals with ethical practices

Aligning business goals with ethical practices is a nuanced endeavor that resonates profoundly with the moral and philosophical teachings of the Mahabharata, an epic that illustrates the complexities of duty, righteousness, and human relationships, providing a rich tapestry of lessons for contemporary organizations seeking to navigate the challenges of ethical governance. At the heart of the Mahabharata is the concept of Dharma, which emphasizes the importance of fulfilling one's duties while adhering to principles of justice and moral integrity; this concept is crucial for businesses aiming to develop a robust ethical framework that guides their operations. Just as Yudhishthira, the eldest Pandava, struggles with the weight of his responsibilities and the moral dilemmas that arise from his pursuit of truth and justice, businesses must recognize that aligning their objectives with ethical practices often requires difficult decisions that prioritize long-term values over short-term gains. Companies can draw inspiration from his character by cultivating a corporate culture that promotes transparency and accountability, ensuring that all stakeholders, from employees to customers, understand the ethical commitments underpinning the organization's goals. The character of Krishna serves as a pivotal mentor in the epic, guiding Arjuna through his moral crisis; similarly, businesses should seek to establish mentorship programs that encourage ethical decision-making at all levels, fostering an environment where employees feel empowered to voice concerns and navigate ethical dilemmas with confidence. This mentorship reflects a broader commitment to ethical leadership, where executives model ethical behavior and prioritize the welfare of their teams, much like Bhishma, who exemplifies loyalty and integrity even in the face of personal sacrifice. Furthermore, the Mahabharata underscores the importance of considering the broader implications of one's actions; businesses can implement ethical practices by integrating corporate social responsibility (CSR) into their strategic planning, recognizing that their decisions impact not only their immediate stakeholders but also the community and environment. This holistic approach can be mirrored in the decisions of characters like Draupadi, who advocates for justice and equity, reminding organizations that ethical practices should extend to fair treatment of all individuals, particularly marginalized groups, thus fostering inclusivity and respect within the workplace. Businesses should also take a page from Karna's story, whose loyalty and ethical struggles reflect the need for alignment between personal values and organizational goals; fostering an inclusive corporate culture where employees can express their values and ethics without fear of retribution encourages a sense of belonging and commitment to the organization's ethical framework. Additionally, the epic illustrates that the pursuit of wealth and success must be balanced with moral considerations, urging businesses to resist the temptation of unethical practices in pursuit of profit, as exemplified by Duryodhana's eventual downfall; this serves as a cautionary tale for organizations that prioritize short-term financial success at the expense of ethical standards. To reinforce this alignment, companies can establish clear ethical guidelines and codes of conduct that resonate with the principles of Dharma, ensuring that employees are aware of the expectations regarding ethical behavior and decision-making processes. Regular training sessions focused on ethical practices, case studies, and the implications of unethical behavior can help instill a strong ethical foundation within the corporate culture, creating a shared understanding of the importance of aligning personal and organizational values. Moreover, businesses can leverage stakeholder engagement as a means to ensure that their goals align with the ethical expectations of the communities they serve; by actively involving stakeholders in decision-making processes, organizations can create a sense of shared responsibility and accountability, reminiscent of the collaborative spirit seen among the Pandavas when they strategize to uphold justice. This engagement can extend to sustainability initiatives, where companies not only comply with regulations but also actively seek to contribute positively to environmental and social issues, embodying the values of responsibility and care that are prevalent in the teachings of the Mahabharata. Transparency in operations, akin to Yudhishthira's commitment to honesty, is essential in building trust with stakeholders; businesses can adopt practices such as open reporting on ethical challenges, progress on sustainability goals, and community contributions to foster an environment of trust and integrity. Furthermore, businesses must be prepared to confront ethical challenges head-on, drawing parallels with the courage exhibited by the characters in the Mahabharata who faced adversity with conviction; organizations should establish whistleblower policies that protect employees who report unethical behavior, thus promoting a culture where ethical concerns can be raised without fear of retaliation. As the Mahabharata emphasizes the importance of wisdom and foresight, businesses should also incorporate ethical considerations into their strategic planning processes, anticipating potential ethical dilemmas and preparing proactive measures to address them. This foresight not only protects the organization from reputational damage but also positions it as a leader in ethical business practices, demonstrating that success can be achieved through integrity and social responsibility. Finally, the Mahabharata teaches that true success is not measured solely by financial gains but by the positive impact one has on society; businesses should evaluate their performance through a dual lens of profitability and ethical contribution, ensuring that their goals reflect a commitment to the greater good. By weaving together these lessons from the Mahabharata, businesses can create a comprehensive framework that aligns their goals with ethical practices, fostering a culture of integrity, responsibility, and respect that not only enhances their reputation but also contributes to a more just and equitable society, ultimately paving the way for sustainable success in the contemporary corporate landscape.

CHAPTER THREE

Leadership

Leadership Lessons from Dhritharashtra and Pandu

The leadership lessons drawn from Dhritarashtra and Pandu in the Mahabharata provide profound insights into the nature of power, responsibility, and moral integrity, illustrating how personal qualities and ethical frameworks shape the destinies of individuals and their communities. Dhritarashtra, the blind king of Hastinapura, epitomizes the challenges of leadership characterized by a lack of vision, both literally and figuratively. His blindness symbolizes not only a physical incapacity but also a moral failing—an inability to perceive the consequences of his actions and the unfolding tensions between his sons, the Kauravas, and their cousins, the Pandavas. Dhritarashtra's leadership style is heavily influenced by his emotions, particularly his deep affection for his sons, which ultimately clouds his judgment. His favoritism toward the Kauravas, particularly Duryodhana, leads to a series of disastrous decisions that exacerbate family tensions and set the stage for the catastrophic conflict of the Kurukshetra War. This aspect of his character illustrates a crucial leadership lesson: the dangers of allowing personal attachments and biases to influence decision-making. A leader must cultivate self-awareness and the ability to detach from personal feelings when making choices that impact the greater good. Dhritarashtra's passive leadership, characterized by indecision and moral ambivalence, ultimately contributes to the disintegration of his family and the tragic loss of life in the war, underscoring the importance of proactive engagement and ethical clarity in governance.

In stark contrast, Pandu, though faced with his own set of challenges, represents a different model of leadership marked by a commitment to righteousness and duty. As a king, Pandu embodies the principles of Dharma, understanding that true leadership requires making choices aligned with ethical values, even at a personal cost. His tragic fate, resulting from a curse that prevents him from engaging in physical intimacy, forces him to make a profound decision: he chooses to renounce the throne and his desires for the sake of ensuring a rightful legacy through his sons. This selfless act demonstrates the leadership quality of prioritizing the collective well-being over personal ambition, emphasizing that true leaders must sometimes make sacrifices for the greater good. Pandu's relationship with his sons—the Pandavas—also highlights the importance of mentorship and guidance in nurturing future leaders. He instills in them a sense of responsibility, duty, and moral integrity, preparing them to face the challenges of leadership themselves. His emphasis on ethical conduct serves as a guiding principle that shapes their character and prepares them for the tumultuous events that lie ahead.

The contrasting leadership styles of Dhritarashtra and Pandu invite reflection on the moral dilemmas and responsibilities that come with power. Dhritarashtra's reluctance to take decisive action and his failure to confront the growing hostility between the Pandavas and Kauravas exemplify the pitfalls of passive leadership, where the inability to address pressing issues leads to catastrophic outcomes. His character serves as a warning against complacency and moral blindness, demonstrating that leaders must be vigilant, self-aware, and willing to act in the best interest of their communities. In contrast, Pandu's proactive approach to leadership illustrates the significance of ethical decision-making and the necessity of aligning one's actions with a moral framework. His choices reflect the idea that effective leadership requires not only courage but also a deep understanding of one's responsibilities to others.

Moreover, the relationship dynamics between these two characters shed light on the complexities of familial loyalty and the ethical dilemmas inherent in leadership roles. Dhritarashtra's unwavering loyalty to his sons, even in the face of their unethical behavior, illustrates the potential for personal biases to cloud judgment and hinder effective leadership. His failure to hold Duryodhana accountable for his actions contributes to the escalation of conflict and the eventual tragedy that befalls both families. This highlights a crucial lesson: leaders must balance loyalty to their loved ones with a commitment to justice and ethical conduct. In contrast, Pandu's actions exemplify the importance of maintaining ethical standards while navigating familial relationships. His decision to ensure the birth of virtuous sons through the practice of niyoga reflects a dedication to ensuring a righteous legacy, even in the face of personal sacrifice. This approach underscores the need for leaders to prioritize ethical considerations over personal desires, reinforcing the idea that leadership is inherently linked to a broader moral responsibility.

The Mahabharata illustrates how the legacies of Dhritarashtra and Pandu serve as a reflection of the broader societal values and ethical frameworks within which they operate. Dhritarashtra's reign is marked by a culture of entitlement and power struggles, exemplified by the Kauravas' relentless pursuit of dominance. This toxic environment fosters unethical behavior and a disregard for justice, ultimately leading to the war that decimates both sides. In contrast, Pandu's leadership promotes values of righteousness, fairness, and accountability, setting a standard that his sons strive to uphold. This dynamic emphasizes the role of leaders in shaping the ethical climate of their organizations or communities, illustrating that leadership are not merely about wielding power but also about cultivating a culture that prioritizes integrity and justice.

The narrative of the Mahabharata further challenges contemporary leaders to reflect on their own values and the impact of their decisions on their teams and organizations. Dhritarashtra's failures serve as a reminder of the consequences of neglecting ethical responsibilities and the importance of holding oneself accountable for the decisions made. In contrast, Pandu's example encourages leaders to embrace their duties with courage and integrity, even when faced with adversity. The lessons gleaned from their leadership journeys resonate with modern discussions on ethical governance, emphasizing the necessity for leaders to cultivate self-awareness, prioritize the greater good, and navigate the complexities of familial and organizational relationships with a commitment to moral principles.

The contrasting leadership lessons from Dhritarashtra and Pandu in the Mahabharata provide a timeless framework for understanding the intricacies of power, responsibility, and ethical decision-making. Their narratives underscore the idea that effective leadership is not defined solely by authority but is rooted in the ability to navigate moral complexities with integrity, courage, and a profound commitment to the welfare of others. By reflecting on their legacies, contemporary leaders can gain valuable insights into the qualities that define effective leadership, recognizing that the path to success is often fraught with ethical dilemmas that require careful consideration, self-reflection, and a steadfast commitment to righteousness. Through the lens of the Mahabharata, the exploration of leadership is not only a study of power dynamics but also an examination of the human condition, emphasizing that true leadership ultimately lies in the choices one makes in the pursuit of justice, integrity, and the greater good.

Dhritharashtra's Blindness - Leadership Failures

Dhritarashtra's blindness in the Mahabharata serves as a powerful metaphor for his profound leadership failures, illustrating how personal flaws and emotional biases can severely undermine effective governance. As the blind king of Hastinapura, Dhritarashtra is unable to see the physical world around him, but his blindness extends far beyond the literal; it represents his inability to perceive the moral and ethical implications of his actions and the dire consequences of his decisions. This lack of vision manifests in his favoritism towards his sons, the Kauravas, particularly Duryodhana, leading him to overlook their unethical behavior and the mounting tensions between the Kauravas and their cousins, the Pandavas. Dhritarashtra's emotional attachments and deep-seated desire to see his sons succeed overshadow his duty as a king, causing him to ignore the principles of justice and fairness that are essential for effective leadership. His indecisiveness and reluctance to confront the growing animosity between the two factions ultimately culminate in the catastrophic Kurukshetra War, showcasing how a leader's inability to act decisively in the face of moral dilemmas can lead to disastrous outcomes. Furthermore, his blindness to the truth reflects a broader failure to engage with the realities of his kingdom; he relies heavily on the counsel of others, particularly his advisor Shakuni, who manipulates the situation to serve his own interests, further illustrating the dangers of poor leadership characterized by dependency on deceitful advisors. This dynamic emphasizes the importance of self-awareness and moral integrity in leadership; Dhritarashtra's failure to acknowledge his limitations and seek counsel from wise and ethical sources ultimately isolates him from the realities of governance, leading to a deterioration of his authority and credibility. Additionally, his inability to reconcile his familial loyalties with his responsibilities as a ruler highlights the complexities of leadership that require a delicate balance between personal emotions and the greater good. This internal conflict results in a paralysis of action, where Dhritarashtra chooses to remain passive rather than make difficult decisions that could have prevented the escalation of conflict. The consequences of his blindness are tragic, as the epic illustrates the devastating effects of his failures not only on his own family but also on the entire kingdom, leading to widespread destruction and loss of life. Ultimately, Dhritarashtra's leadership failures serve as a cautionary tale about the dangers of moral blindness, emphasizing that effective leadership requires clarity of vision, a commitment to justice, and the courage to act decisively in the face of ethical challenges. His character embodies the idea that leaders must cultivate self-awareness and the ability to engage with the complexities of their roles, recognizing that true leadership demands not only authority but also the ability to navigate the intricate moral landscapes that define their responsibilities.

Analysis of ineffective leadership styles in corporations

An analysis of ineffective leadership styles in corporations through the lens of the Mahabharata reveals profound insights into the pitfalls of various approaches to leadership, emphasizing how personal flaws and ethical failures can lead to organizational dysfunction and conflict. In the epic, characters such as Dhritarashtra exemplify the dangers of passive leadership, where indecision and moral blindness result in catastrophic consequences. Dhritarashtra's favoritism toward his sons, particularly Duryodhana, leads him to overlook unethical behaviors and create an environment ripe for conflict, mirroring how corporate leaders who prioritize personal relationships over ethical standards can undermine organizational integrity. This type of leadership often fosters a toxic culture where loyalty is valued over competence, resulting in a lack of accountability and transparency. Similarly, the character of Shakuni serves as a cautionary tale about manipulative leadership, as his self-serving tactics exploit Dhritarashtra's weaknesses, illustrating how leaders who engage in deceit and manipulation can create discord and instability within an organization. This reflects a broader issue in corporate environments where leaders may prioritize short-term gains over long-term sustainability, compromising ethical standards for personal advantage. Furthermore, the ineffective leadership of Duryodhana, marked by arrogance and a relentless pursuit of power, exemplifies how egocentric leadership can lead to an environment of fear and resentment. Duryodhana's unwillingness to engage in dialogue or consider alternative perspectives results in a breakdown of communication, stifling collaboration and innovation. This parallels corporate cultures where leaders adopt authoritarian styles, fostering a culture of silence where employees feel disempowered to voice their ideas or concerns, ultimately stifling growth and creativity. Additionally, the character of Karna reflects the consequences of misplaced loyalty and ethical ambiguity in leadership; his unwavering allegiance to Duryodhana, despite knowing the latter's moral failings, illustrates how loyalty can cloud judgment and lead to complicity in unethical practices. In corporate settings, leaders who prioritize loyalty over ethical considerations can inadvertently cultivate a culture of compliance rather than accountability, where employees may feel pressured to conform to unethical practices out of fear of repercussions. The tragic outcomes of the Kurukshetra War serve as a poignant reminder of the collective consequences of ineffective leadership styles, emphasizing that poor decision-making at the top can reverberate throughout an organization, leading to widespread dysfunction and failure. The Mahabharata thus serves as a timeless reflection on the complexities of leadership, illustrating the necessity for leaders to cultivate self-awareness, ethical integrity, and a commitment to fostering an inclusive and collaborative culture. By analyzing these characters and their leadership styles, modern organizations can glean valuable lessons about the importance of ethical leadership, the dangers of manipulation and favoritism, and the critical need for open communication and accountability in creating a healthy organizational environment that promotes long-term success and sustainability.

Pandu's Enlightened Leadership

Pandu's enlightened leadership in the Mahabharata represents a profound exploration of ethical governance, moral integrity, and the responsibilities that accompany power, providing timeless lessons relevant to contemporary leadership practices. As the king of Hastinapura, Pandu is faced with immense challenges, including a tragic curse that prevents him from enjoying the marital pleasures of kingship, ultimately compelling him to abdicate traditional notions of power in favor of a more principled approach to leadership. His enlightened perspective is characterized by a deep understanding of Dharma, or righteous duty, which guides his decisions and actions throughout his life. Unlike his brother Dhritarashtra, whose emotional blindness leads to favoritism and conflict, Pandu embodies a sense of moral clarity and selflessness, prioritizing the well-being of his family and kingdom over personal desires. This is most vividly illustrated in his choice to father children through the practice of niyoga, enabling him to fulfill his royal duty while navigating the complexities of his curse. Through this decision, Pandu demonstrates a commitment to ensuring a righteous legacy, emphasizing the importance of duty and responsibility in leadership. His relationship with his sons, the Pandavas, further underscores his enlightened approach; he instills in them values of integrity, compassion, and respect, nurturing their character and preparing them to face the moral complexities of leadership themselves. Pandu's efforts to foster an environment of openness and ethical conduct create a foundation for the Pandavas, who embody the virtues of courage and righteousness as they navigate their own trials. Additionally, Pandu's ability to confront his limitations and make sacrifices for the greater good illustrates a key trait of enlightened leadership: humility. Rather than succumbing to bitterness over his curse, he embraces his fate with dignity, recognizing that true power lies not in personal gratification but in the impact one has on others. This aspect of his character emphasizes that effective leaders must possess emotional intelligence, allowing them to navigate adversity with grace and integrity. Furthermore, Pandu's proactive approach to governance, where he prioritizes the welfare of his subjects and seeks to uphold justice, positions him as a figure of moral authority within the epic. He stands as a counterpoint to the toxic leadership exhibited by Dhritarashtra and the Kauravas, demonstrating that enlightened leadership requires a balance of strength and compassion. Ultimately, Pandu's enlightened leadership serves as a beacon for contemporary leaders, reminding them of the importance of ethical decision-making, self-awareness, and the need to foster a culture of integrity and accountability within their organizations. His legacy, defined by a commitment to righteousness and the well-being of others, invites modern leaders to reflect on their values and the lasting impact of their choices, reinforcing the idea that true leadership is grounded in the principles of justice, duty, and the welfare of the community.

Qualities of a good leader: empathy, vision, and moral integrity

In the Mahabharata, the qualities of a good leader—empathy, vision, and moral integrity—are vividly illustrated through various characters and their actions, offering timeless lessons on effective leadership that resonate in contemporary contexts. Empathy, as depicted in the epic, is crucial for leaders who must navigate complex interpersonal dynamics, understand the needs and emotions of their subjects, and create a sense of community. This quality is especially embodied by Yudhishthira, the eldest of the Pandavas, whose deep sense of compassion and fairness shapes his approach to leadership. Yudhishthira's empathy allows him to connect with others on a personal level, making him approachable and relatable as a leader. For instance, throughout the epic, he demonstrates a profound understanding of the suffering of others, whether it is during the trials of his family or the hardships faced by his subjects. His interactions with characters such as Draupadi, whom he respects and supports during her time of need, reflect his ability to empathize with the plight of others. This quality is essential for fostering trust and loyalty among followers, as leaders who exhibit empathy are more likely to inspire a sense of belonging and commitment within their communities.

Vision is another fundamental quality that distinguishes effective leaders in the Mahabharata. A leader must possess the foresight to anticipate future challenges and opportunities while articulating a clear and inspiring direction for their followers. This visionary quality is notably exemplified by Krishna, who plays a pivotal role as a guide and strategist throughout the epic. His ability to perceive the broader implications of the unfolding events and to communicate a sense of purpose to the Pandavas highlights the importance of having a visionary leader in times of crisis. Krishna's counsel to Arjuna on the battlefield of Kurukshetra serves as a profound moment of clarity, where he not only addresses Arjuna's doubts and fears but also frames the conflict in the context of Dharma and righteousness. This moment underscores the significance of having a leader who can provide a coherent vision, instilling courage and motivation in followers when they are faced with uncertainty. A visionary leader not only defines the path forward but also inspires others to engage in the shared pursuit of a common goal, fostering unity and resilience among their followers.

Moral integrity is perhaps the most critical quality that underpins effective leadership in the Mahabharata. Leaders must uphold ethical standards and principles, even when faced with difficult choices and temptations. This quality is epitomized by characters like Bhishma and Yudhishthira, who, despite the immense pressures and moral dilemmas they encounter, remain steadfast in their commitment to righteousness. Bhishma's vow of celibacy and his unwavering loyalty to the Kuru dynasty exemplify his moral integrity, as he prioritizes duty over personal desires. His adherence to principles, even at great personal cost, establishes him as a moral compass within the epic, and his counsel is often sought for guidance in matters of ethics and justice. Yudhishthira, too, embodies moral integrity, particularly in his insistence on honesty and truthfulness, even when it leads to dire consequences for himself and his family. His infamous gamble, which results in the loss of everything, reflects the complexity of moral decisions in leadership; he chooses to adhere to his principles, illustrating that moral integrity often requires making sacrifices for the sake of upholding one's values.

These three qualities—empathy, vision, and moral integrity—are interrelated and collectively shape the effectiveness of a leader. A leader who possesses empathy can better understand the aspirations and concerns of their followers, allowing them to craft a vision that resonates deeply with the collective desires of the community. Likewise, a strong moral compass ensures that the vision articulated by a leader is rooted in ethical principles, fostering trust and commitment among followers. In the Mahabharata, the interplay of these qualities becomes apparent through the actions and choices of the various characters, illustrating the diverse approaches to leadership and their consequences.

For instance, Dhritarashtra's leadership is marked by a lack of vision and moral integrity, compounded by his emotional blindness. His favoritism towards his sons leads to a culture of entitlement and injustice, ultimately culminating in conflict and tragedy. In contrast, the qualities embodied by Pandu, Yudhishthira, and Krishna highlight the necessity of empathy, vision, and moral integrity in leadership. Their collective experiences underscore that effective leadership is not merely a matter of authority but is fundamentally rooted in the ability to connect with others, to inspire a shared vision, and to uphold ethical standards in the face of adversity.

The Mahabharata also serves as a cautionary tale about the consequences of leadership devoid of these essential qualities. Characters like Duryodhana and Shakuni exemplify the dangers of ambition and manipulation when empathy, vision, and moral integrity are absent. Duryodhana's relentless pursuit of power, characterized by his willingness to engage in deceit and moral ambiguity, leads to a devastating conflict that destroys his family and kingdom. His inability to empathize with the Pandavas and his refusal to acknowledge their rightful claims demonstrate how a lack of understanding and compassion can erode the foundations of effective leadership. Shakuni, as a manipulative strategist, exemplifies the consequences of prioritizing personal gain over the welfare of others. His cunning tactics and lack of ethical considerations create an environment rife with distrust and conflict, ultimately contributing to the tragic outcomes of the war.

Through the lens of the Mahabharata, the qualities of good leadership can also be examined within the context of contemporary organizational dynamics. In today's fast-paced and complex environments, leaders are faced with myriad challenges that require them to navigate competing interests while maintaining a commitment to ethical principles. Empathy plays a vital role in fostering inclusive workplaces where individuals feel valued and heard.

Leaders who practice empathy can create cultures of collaboration, where diverse perspectives are acknowledged and integrated into decision-making processes. This not only enhances employee engagement but also drives innovation and adaptability, essential qualities for success in a rapidly changing world.

Vision remains equally critical in contemporary leadership, as organizations must continuously evolve to meet the demands of their markets and stakeholders. Leaders with a clear and compelling vision can galvanize their teams, fostering a sense of purpose and direction that inspires collective action. Visionary leaders are adept at communicating their goals and aspirations in ways that resonate with their followers, encouraging them to invest their energies in the pursuit of shared objectives. Furthermore, the ability to anticipate future trends and challenges enables leaders to position their organizations strategically, fostering resilience and sustainability in the face of uncertainty.

Moral integrity is the cornerstone of effective leadership, particularly in an era marked by increasing scrutiny and demand for accountability. Leaders who exemplify moral integrity inspire trust and loyalty among their followers, cultivating a culture of transparency and ethical behavior. In a world where ethical dilemmas often arise, leaders with a strong moral compass can guide their organizations through difficult decisions, reinforcing the importance of doing what is right over what is expedient. The Mahabharata's emphasis on moral integrity serves as a reminder that ethical leadership is not only about adhering to rules but also about embodying values that resonate with the broader community.

The interplay of empathy, vision, and moral integrity in the Mahabharata ultimately underscores the idea that leadership is a complex and multifaceted endeavor. Characters such as Yudhishthira, Krishna, and Bhishma exemplify the profound impact of these qualities on their effectiveness as leaders, demonstrating that true leadership is about more than authority; it is about the ability to inspire, uplift, and guide others toward a common goal while upholding ethical principles. As we reflect on the lessons drawn from this epic, it becomes clear that cultivating empathy, fostering a visionary mindset, and maintaining moral integrity are essential components of effective leadership that transcend time and context.

As Mahabharata serves as a rich source of insights into the qualities that define good leadership, with empathy, vision, and moral integrity emerging as foundational elements, the characters within the epic provide compelling examples of how these qualities can manifest in different contexts, illustrating the profound impact they have on the outcomes of their choices and actions. As contemporary leaders grapple with the complexities of their roles, the lessons embedded in the Mahabharata offer valuable guidance on the path to effective and ethical leadership. By embodying these qualities, leaders can cultivate environments that promote trust, collaboration, and accountability, ultimately fostering a culture where individuals can thrive and contribute to the greater good. The timeless wisdom of the Mahabharata thus reinforces the idea that the essence of true leadership lies not only in the pursuit of power but in the commitment to serve others with empathy, clarity of vision, and unwavering moral integrity.

✿

CHAPTER FOUR

Gender Dynamics

The Role of Women - Draupadi as a Figure of Empowerment

Draupadi's role in the Mahabharata serves as a profound illustration of female empowerment, embodying resilience, agency, and the complexities of womanhood in a patriarchal society. As the daughter of King Drupada, her birth is marked by a prophecy that she would be pivotal in the downfall of the Kauravas, setting the stage for her to emerge as a central figure in the epic. Draupadi's multifaceted character challenges traditional gender roles; she is not merely a passive recipient of fate but an active agent whose choices and actions significantly influence the narrative. Her marriage to the five Pandavas—Yudhishthira, Bhima, Arjuna, Nakula, and Sahadeva—illustrates her unique position as a woman who navigates the complexities of polygamy with grace and intelligence, advocating for her rights and the dignity of her family. One of the most critical moments showcasing her empowerment occurs during the infamous dice game, where she is publicly humiliated and stripped of her dignity by Duryodhana and his brothers. Instead of succumbing to despair, Draupadi's response to this violation becomes a defining moment of resistance; she raises her voice against injustice and calls upon Krishna for protection, embodying the struggle for honor and justice. This incident highlights her refusal to accept subjugation, reflecting the broader themes of empowerment and agency for women in the Mahabharata. Furthermore, Draupadi's ability to articulate her grievances and assert her dignity in a male-dominated society signifies her role as a powerful figure who challenges patriarchal norms. Her relationship with the Pandavas is also significant; she serves not only as a wife but as a confidante and strategist, influencing their decisions and standing as a moral compass for them. This dynamic illustrates that women in the Mahabharata are not relegated to mere background roles; they are integral to the narrative's progression and moral discourse. Draupadi's character challenges the notion of women as passive victims, instead portraying them as strong individuals with the capacity to shape their destinies. Moreover, her quest for justice and equality resonates with contemporary discussions on women's rights and empowerment, making her an enduring symbol of strength. Throughout the epic, Draupadi navigates the challenges of societal expectations while maintaining her individuality and self-worth, advocating for the rights of women and reflecting the complexities of female identity. Her fiery spirit and resilience stand in stark contrast to the limitations imposed on her by societal norms, allowing her to transcend her role as a queen and become a leader in her own right. The portrayal of Draupadi culminates in her refusal to remain silent in the face of injustice, marking her as a figure of empowerment who inspires future generations to challenge oppressive structures. Her ultimate vindication, when she is honored and respected by the Pandavas and Krishna during the war, signifies the triumph of justice and the restoration of dignity, reinforcing the notion that women, when empowered, can challenge the status quo and redefine their roles in society. Thus, Draupadi's journey within the Mahabharata not only illustrates the struggles of women in a patriarchal context but also serves as a powerful narrative of empowerment, resilience, and the enduring strength of the female spirit, resonating deeply with contemporary themes of gender equality and the ongoing quest for women's rights. Her character remains a testament to the idea that empowerment is not merely about status or privilege but about the ability to assert one's dignity, voice, and agency in the face of adversity, inspiring countless women to fight for justice and equality in their own lives.

Gender Dynamics in the Mahabharata

Gender dynamics in the Mahabharata present a complex interplay of power, agency, and societal expectations that offer profound insights into the roles and representations of women in ancient Indian society. The epic features a rich tapestry of characters, each illustrating various aspects of gender relations, often reflecting the tensions between patriarchal structures and the assertion of female agency. Central to these dynamics is Draupadi, whose multifaceted character exemplifies both the limitations imposed on women and their capacity for empowerment. Born from fire and destined to play a pivotal role in the epic's narrative, Draupadi's journey begins with her marriage to the five Pandavas, a union that itself challenges conventional notions of marriage and gender roles. Her position as a shared wife defies singular ownership, suggesting a broader understanding of female agency and partnership, yet she also grapples with the consequences of being a pawn in the power struggles between men. The infamous game of dice highlights the precariousness of her status; her public humiliation serves as a stark commentary on the vulnerabilities women face in patriarchal societies. Yet, Draupadi's response to this injustice—her invocation of Krishna's divine support and her unwavering demand for dignity—transforms her into a symbol of resistance and empowerment.

Alongside Draupadi, other female characters in the Mahabharata, such as Kunti and Gandhari, also contribute to the discourse on gender dynamics. Kunti, the mother of the Pandavas, embodies maternal sacrifice and strength, often navigating the complexities of her relationships with her sons and her co-wives. Her actions demonstrate how women exert influence behind the scenes, managing familial relationships and ensuring the welfare of their children, thus highlighting the pivotal yet often invisible roles women play within the family structure. In contrast, Gandhari, the mother of the Kauravas, presents a different dimension of womanhood. Her blindfold symbolizes both her loyalty to her husband and her awareness of the moral failings of her sons, reflecting the tragic consequences of parental love when intertwined with ambition and conflict. Her character invites reflection on the sacrifices women make in the name of familial loyalty, often at the expense of their own agency. The epic also addresses the societal expectations placed upon women, particularly concerning honor, purity, and loyalty. Women like Draupadi and Kunti are often defined by their relationships to men—be it as wives, mothers, or daughters—which raises questions about the nature of their identity and autonomy. Draupadi's challenge to patriarchal norms, especially in her fierce assertion of dignity and justice, serves as a counter-narrative to traditional gender roles. Her character resonates with contemporary issues of gender inequality, inspiring discussions about women's rights and agency in the modern world. Furthermore, the relationships between male characters often reflect the ways in which women are objectified or marginalized within the narrative. The rivalry between the Pandavas and Kauravas, rooted in ambition and desire for power, often places women in the crossfire, revealing the ways in which their fates are determined by the actions of men. The dynamics of power in the epic illustrate how gender intersects with social hierarchies, emphasizing that women's worth is frequently measured by their ability to conform to patriarchal expectations. The representation of female characters in the Mahabharata also raises critical questions about the nature of virtue and morality. Women are often tasked with upholding familial honor, yet they are subjected to harsh judgments based on their adherence to societal norms. This duality creates a paradox where women are both revered and reviled, illustrating the complexities of gender roles. The epic's treatment of characters like Surpanakha, who is vilified for her desires and ambitions, further underscores the harsh scrutiny women face. Her transformation into a demoness after being spurned by Rama exemplifies how women's desires are often demonized within patriarchal narratives, reinforcing negative stereotypes about female ambition and autonomy.

In addition to individual characters, the Mahabharata presents a broader commentary on the interplay between gender and power in society. The epic portrays the consequences of male aggression and the resulting conflicts, often positioning women as collateral damage in the battles for dominance. However, women like Draupadi do not remain passive; instead, they assert their agency, challenging the patriarchal structures that seek to confine them. Draupadi's call for justice during the dice game becomes a rallying point for both her own empowerment and a critique of the systemic injustices faced by women. Her unwavering stance against her oppressors highlights the potential for women to reclaim their power and influence the course of events. The Mahabharata also explores the concept of dharma, or righteous duty, and how it intersects with gender roles. The expectations placed on women to uphold family honor often conflict with their personal desires and autonomy, creating moral dilemmas that resonate throughout the epic. Characters like Kunti and Draupadi navigate these complexities, embodying the struggle between societal expectations and individual agency. The concept of dharma thus serves as both a guiding principle and a source of conflict for women, who must balance their responsibilities to family and society with their personal aspirations.

The portrayal of women in the Mahabharata ultimately reflects the intricate web of gender dynamics that define the epic. While women like Draupadi and Kunti navigate their roles within a patriarchal framework, they also exemplify the capacity for agency, resilience, and empowerment. Their stories serve as reminders of the multifaceted nature of womanhood, challenging simplistic narratives that reduce women to passive figures. The dynamics between male and female characters illustrate the power struggles inherent in the epic, revealing how women's fates are often entangled with the ambitions and desires of men. Gender dynamics in the Mahabharata are rich and multifaceted, encompassing themes of power, agency, and societal expectations. Characters like Draupadi, Kunti, and Gandhari challenge conventional notions of femininity and virtue, asserting their voices and influencing the course of events despite the constraints of a patriarchal society. The epic serves as a profound commentary on the complexities of gender roles, illustrating the struggles women face in navigating their identities while contending with societal norms. Draupadi's journey, in particular, resonates with contemporary discussions about gender equality, highlighting the enduring relevance of her story in the ongoing quest for women's rights and empowerment. The Mahabharata invites readers to reflect on the intricate interplay of gender and power, ultimately emphasizing those women, when empowered, can challenge and reshape the narratives that seek to define them.

Draupadi's strength and resilience

Draupadi's strength and resilience in the Mahabharata encapsulate her as a formidable figure whose journey reflects profound themes of empowerment, justice, and agency amidst a patriarchal society. Born from the fire, Draupadi's very existence signifies her extraordinary destiny, heralded by a prophecy that she would play a crucial role in the downfall of the Kauravas. Her marriage to the five Pandavas—a union that defies traditional norms of monogamy—positions her uniquely as both a wife and a partner, emphasizing her strength in navigating complex relationships and asserting her identity within them. However, her trials reach a harrowing peak during the infamous game of dice, where she is wagered and subsequently humiliated in the Kaurava court. This moment becomes a defining test of her character; rather than succumbing to despair, Draupadi's resilience shines through as she fiercely confronts her captors, demanding justice and invoking Krishna's divine intervention for protection. This act of defiance not only showcases her courage but also her refusal to be reduced to mere property in a male-dominated society. Draupadi's emotional strength is equally compelling; after her public humiliation, she emerges as a beacon of dignity and resilience, supporting her husbands during their exile and embodying the spirit of survival. Throughout their trials, she takes on the role of a leader, maintaining the morale of the Pandavas and managing the household, demonstrating that her strength is not merely reactive but proactive, rooted in her unwavering commitment to her family. Her interactions with the Pandavas reveal a complex dynamic where she is not just a passive recipient of their decisions but an assertive partner who challenges their choices and expectations, advocating for her own dignity and that of her family. This complexity is particularly evident in her relationship with Yudhishthira; her confrontation with him after the dice game speaks volumes about her moral fortitude and her insistence on ethical conduct, even when it contradicts the societal norms that dictate her subservience. Draupadi's evolution throughout the Kurukshetra War further solidifies her as a figure of empowerment; the conflict itself, fought over her honor, highlights her centrality in the narrative and her transformation from victim to avenger, as her desire for justice drives the Pandavas to reclaim their rightful place. In the aftermath of the war, Draupadi's character transcends mere vengeance; she stands as a testament to the resilience of women who, despite suffering profound losses, emerge as pillars of strength, advocating for justice and the restoration of dignity. Her journey resonates deeply with contemporary discussions surrounding gender and empowerment, illustrating the timeless struggle for dignity and recognition faced by women in various contexts. Draupadi's ability to reclaim her narrative and assert her agency in a society that seeks to diminish her speaks to the enduring power of resilience and the necessity for women to challenge oppressive structures. Her character not only reflects the complexities of womanhood but also inspires future generations to recognize their own strength, advocating for justice in the face of adversity. Ultimately, Draupadi's story is one of transformation, illustrating that true strength lies not only in physical might but in the courage to stand up against injustice, reclaim one's dignity, and inspire others to do the same, making her one of the most iconic and empowering figures in the Mahabharata and a symbol of female resilience that continues to inspire and resonate today.

Women in Contemporary Business

Women in contemporary business can draw profound insights from the narratives and characters in the Mahabharata, where themes of resilience, agency, and moral integrity are vividly illustrated through the lives of key female figures such as Draupadi and Kunti. In a world where women often face systemic barriers in professional environments, the strength and adaptability of Draupadi, particularly in the face of adversity, serve as powerful reminders of the potential for female empowerment. Draupadi's story begins with her birth from fire, symbolizing resilience and a unique destiny that positions her as a catalyst for change; similarly, modern women in business are increasingly taking on pivotal roles that challenge traditional norms and expectations. Her experience during the infamous dice game—where she is humiliated but responds with courage—highlights the importance of standing up against injustice, a lesson that resonates with women today who often navigate male-dominated corporate landscapes. The way she articulates her demands for justice and respect illustrates the need for women to assert their voices and rights in business settings, advocating for equity and ethical practices. Kunti, another significant figure, embodies the qualities of sacrifice and moral integrity, showing that leadership is not solely about authority but also about fostering relationships and nurturing those around you. Her ability to balance her responsibilities as a mother and a leader speaks to the challenges contemporary women face in harmonizing professional aspirations with familial duties, reinforcing the idea that nurturing qualities can coexist with ambitious professional pursuits. Additionally, the relationships between male and female characters in the Mahabharata emphasize the necessity of mutual respect and collaboration in achieving success, reflecting modern concepts of teamwork and partnership in business. The dynamics of power and ethics depicted in the epic remind women today of the importance of cultivating a strong moral compass in their professional journeys, ensuring that they not only pursue success but do so with integrity and accountability. As women in contemporary business confront challenges such as gender bias, wage gaps, and the struggle for representation in leadership roles, the narratives of the Mahabharata serve as a source of inspiration, highlighting the need for resilience, strategic thinking, and the courage to advocate for oneself and others. Draupadi's unwavering resolve to reclaim her dignity in the face of public humiliation serves as a powerful metaphor for the modern woman's fight against discrimination and inequality in the workplace, urging them to harness their voices and agency to effect change. Furthermore, the epic illustrates the importance of mentorship and solidarity among women, as seen in the supportive relationships that exist among female characters, encouraging contemporary women to build networks of empowerment that foster growth and success. Ultimately, the lessons derived from the Mahabharata underscore that women in contemporary business must embrace their strength, navigate challenges with resilience, and advocate for a more equitable workplace, echoing the enduring themes of empowerment and justice that resonate through the epic's narrative. By embodying the qualities exemplified by Draupadi and Kunti—strength, moral integrity, and the courage to challenge societal norms—women today can forge paths of leadership that not only advance their own careers but also contribute to a more inclusive and just business environment. The Mahabharata's portrayal of women as multifaceted characters who actively shape their destinies serves as a timeless reminder that female empowerment is essential for progress, urging contemporary women to recognize their inherent strength and capacity to lead, innovate, and inspire in the ever-evolving landscape of business.

The importance of women in leadership roles and corporate policies

The importance of women in leadership roles and corporate policies can be profoundly understood through the lens of the Mahabharata, an epic that intricately weaves narratives of power, agency, and the pivotal roles women play in shaping the moral and ethical fabric of society. Central to this discourse is Draupadi, whose character embodies resilience, intelligence, and a profound understanding of justice and honor. As a woman who stands at the intersection of personal dignity and political intrigue, Draupadi's experiences reflect the necessity of female voices in leadership positions. Her role is not merely that of a passive participant in the events that unfold; rather, she emerges as a catalyst for change, advocating for her rights and challenging the patriarchal structures that seek to diminish her worth. In modern corporate environments, the inclusion of women in leadership roles is essential for fostering diverse perspectives and innovative solutions. Just as Draupadi's courage and resolve inspire the Pandavas to reclaim their rightful place and fight for justice, women in leadership today drive organizations toward more ethical practices and inclusive policies that benefit all stakeholders

The Mahabharata also highlights the complex relationships between men and women and the importance of collaboration in leadership. Characters such as Kunti and Gandhari exemplify different aspects of female strength and moral integrity, offering lessons on the value of empathy and support in leadership. Kunti, as the mother of the Pandavas, embodies nurturing qualities while simultaneously exercising strategic thinking and foresight in navigating familial dynamics. Her role in ensuring her sons' success while maintaining the family's honor illustrates how women can balance emotional intelligence with decision-making capabilities, an essential trait for effective leadership in contemporary corporate settings. Similarly, Gandhari, though often perceived through the lens of tragedy, demonstrates unwavering loyalty and moral strength, reflecting the sacrifices women make for the sake of their families and communities. These narratives underscore the idea that women's leadership is not solely about authority but also about fostering relationships, nurturing talent, and creating environments where ethical considerations thrive.

In the context of corporate policies, the Mahabharata's teachings on dharma, or righteousness, resonate deeply with the need for ethical governance and responsible leadership. Draupadi's insistence on justice during her public humiliation serves as a powerful reminder of the importance of accountability and ethical standards in any leadership role. Her refusal to accept injustice, even in the face of overwhelming odds, speaks to the role women must play in advocating for ethical practices within organizations. When women occupy leadership positions, they bring unique perspectives that challenge the status quo and encourage organizations to adopt policies that prioritize fairness, inclusion, and transparency. Research consistently shows that companies with diverse leadership teams are more innovative and better equipped to adapt to changing market conditions. This parallels Draupadi's multifaceted character—she is a warrior, a queen, and a strategist—demonstrating that women can excel in various roles while contributing to holistic decision-making processes. Mahabharata illustrates the consequences of power when wielded without ethical consideration. The Kauravas, particularly Duryodhana, embody a leadership style characterized by ambition and ruthlessness, leading to destructive outcomes for themselves and their allies. In contrast, the Pandavas, guided by Draupadi's moral compass and Kunti's nurturing yet strategic approach, illustrate the effectiveness of ethical leadership grounded in integrity and respect. This dichotomy serves as a cautionary tale for contemporary organizations, emphasizing the need for women in leadership who can advocate for policies that align with ethical practices and social responsibility. The stories of the Mahabharata remind us that leadership is not just about achieving success; it is about ensuring that the path to success does not compromise ethical standards or the well-being of others. In this light, the inclusion of women in leadership roles is vital to fostering a culture of accountability and ethical decision-making.

The epic underscores the importance of mentorship and solidarity among women, a theme that resonates with modern corporate structures. The relationships between female characters in the Mahabharata, such as Draupadi's camaraderie with her co-wives and her interactions with other women, reflect the strength that emerges from support networks. These relationships provide not only emotional resilience but also strategic alliances that empower women to navigate challenges more effectively. In contemporary business environments, fostering a culture of mentorship among women can lead to enhanced leadership development and increased representation in decision-making roles. When women support one another, they create a ripple effect that encourages the next generation of female leaders to step forward and assert their agency, much like Draupadi's insistence on her dignity inspires the Pandavas to act justly. Moreover, the Mahabharata emphasizes the significance of women's voices in shaping societal values and norms. As Draupadi publicly confronts the Kauravas, she does not merely seek personal vengeance; she seeks to redefine the boundaries of honor and justice, challenging the patriarchal norms that dictate her worth. This act of defiance is not just a personal struggle; it is a broader commentary on the systemic inequalities that women face. In the corporate world, when women hold leadership roles, they can influence policies that address issues such as gender discrimination, workplace harassment, and inequitable pay. Their unique experiences and insights enable them to advocate for initiatives that promote inclusivity and equality, fostering environments where all employees can thrive. The Mahabharata's emphasis on the power of dialogue and discourse is echoed in the need for open communication channels within organizations, where diverse perspectives are valued and heard.

The legacy of the Mahabharata ultimately serves as a powerful reminder of the potential for women to lead with integrity and courage, transforming not only their own lives but also the lives of those around them. As Draupadi exemplifies, leadership is about more than authority; it is about having the moral courage to stand up for what is right and to inspire others to do the same. This ethos is crucial in contemporary corporate settings, where ethical dilemmas often arise, and the integrity of leadership is put to the test. Women in leadership roles can serve as catalysts for cultural change, driving organizations toward practices that prioritize social responsibility and ethical considerations. By championing policies that reflect these values, they can create workplaces that are not only more equitable but also more sustainable in the long run.

The need of women in leadership roles and corporate policies is stated by the narratives and teachings found in the Mahabharata. Through the characters of Draupadi, Kunti, and Gandhari, the epic illustrates the multifaceted nature of female strength and the essential qualities that women bring to leadership. Their stories emphasize the significance of ethical governance, mentorship, and the courage to challenge societal norms. In contemporary business, women leaders are crucial for fostering inclusive policies, driving ethical practices, and creating environments where diverse voices are heard and valued. The lessons drawn from the Mahabharata remind us that the empowerment of women is not just a matter of equity; it is essential for the health and sustainability of organizations and society as a whole. As we look to the future, embracing and promoting women in leadership roles will be vital for creating a more just and equitable world, ensuring that the values of integrity, resilience, and collaboration are upheld in every facet of our professional lives.

CHAPTER FIVE

Corporate Advisory

The Role of Advisors - Krishna's Guidance

The role of advisors in the Mahabharata, particularly exemplified through Krishna's guidance, is a central theme that highlights the significance of wisdom, strategic thinking, and moral integrity in navigating complex situations. Krishna, often regarded as the divine charioteer and counselor, embodies the qualities of an ideal advisor, demonstrating how critical guidance can shape the course of events and influence outcomes in the epic's narrative. His relationship with the Pandavas, especially with Arjuna, serves as a testament to the importance of mentorship and the necessity of having a wise counselor during times of crisis. At the onset of the Kurukshetra War, Arjuna finds himself in a moral quandary, torn between his duty as a warrior (kshatriya) and his deep emotional ties to his relatives on the opposing side. It is Krishna's profound wisdom and understanding of dharma that provides Arjuna with the clarity he desperately needs. Krishna's teachings encompass not only practical strategies for warfare but also philosophical insights about life, duty, and righteousness, emphasizing the integral role of ethical considerations in decision-making. His counsel encourages Arjuna to rise above personal attachments and to embrace his responsibilities, framing the war as a necessary battle for justice and righteousness. This pivotal moment underscores the vital nature of advisors in shaping the perceptions and actions of leaders; Krishna's ability to impart wisdom allows Arjuna to reclaim his resolve and fulfill his destiny. Moreover, Krishna's role transcends that of a mere strategist; he serves as a moral compass for the Pandavas, guiding them through the complexities of loyalty, honor, and ethical dilemmas that arise throughout the epic. His interventions, whether in diplomatic negotiations or in battlefield strategies, illustrate the multifaceted nature of advisory roles, where the advisor must balance personal loyalties with the larger picture of justice and dharma. Krishna's influence extends beyond the battlefield; his ability to navigate intricate political landscapes, such as orchestrating alliances and defusing potential conflicts, highlights the importance of wise counsel in governance. Through his strategic foresight, Krishna not only aids the Pandavas but also plays a crucial role in shaping the political dynamics of the time, demonstrating that effective leadership is deeply intertwined with sound advice. Additionally, the epic reveals the consequences of ignoring wise counsel, as seen in the Kauravas' decisions, particularly through Duryodhana's choices, which are often influenced by arrogance and a lack of sound guidance. The tragic outcomes that befall the Kauravas serve as a cautionary tale about the importance of seeking and heeding wise advice. In contrast, the Pandavas, despite facing immense challenges, are ultimately able to navigate their path to victory due to their willingness to listen to Krishna and adapt his guidance into their strategies. This dynamic illustrates how leadership is not merely about authority or strength but also about the capacity to seek help and incorporate diverse perspectives into decision-making processes. The Mahabharata thus positions Krishna as a paragon of wisdom, whose counsel is not only practical but also deeply philosophical, urging leaders to reflect on their actions within the broader context of ethical responsibilities and societal implications. His teachings resonate with contemporary leadership principles, highlighting the necessity of moral integrity and the courage to make difficult decisions in the pursuit of justice. Furthermore, Krishna's interactions with various characters in the Mahabharata reveal the complexities of advisory relationships, where trust, respect, and mutual understanding play crucial roles. His ability to engage with both allies and adversaries demonstrates that effective advisors must possess emotional intelligence and adaptability, allowing them to navigate the intricacies of human relationships while guiding their leaders toward sound decisions. This theme is particularly relevant in today's corporate and political landscapes, where the quality of advice can significantly influence organizational success and ethical governance. In conclusion, the role of advisors like Krishna in the Mahabharata emphasizes the importance of wisdom, strategic thinking, and moral integrity in leadership. His guidance shapes the narrative of the epic, illustrating that the effectiveness of leaders often hinges on their willingness to seek and accept counsel. As organizations and leaders today navigate complex challenges, the lessons derived from Krishna's role as an advisor serve as a powerful reminder of the enduring value of sound advice and ethical considerations in shaping outcomes, ultimately underscoring the timeless relevance of the Mahabharata in contemporary discussions about leadership and governance.

The Importance of Mentorship

The importance of mentorship in the Mahabharata is profoundly illustrated through the relationships and guidance that shape the lives of its characters, emphasizing how mentorship serves as a vital force in personal and moral development, strategic decision-making, and the navigation of ethical dilemmas. One of the most significant mentor-mentee relationships in the epic is that between Krishna and Arjuna, which serves as a powerful testament to the transformative impact of wise counsel. At the onset of the Kurukshetra War, Arjuna faces an existential crisis, torn between his duty as a warrior and his emotional ties to family members on the opposing side. In this moment of deep uncertainty, Krishna steps in as his charioteer and guide, providing not only practical strategies for warfare but also profound philosophical teachings on dharma, duty, and righteousness. Krishna's mentorship is characterized by a deep understanding of Arjuna's inner turmoil; he employs a blend of compassion and firmness, helping Arjuna to confront his fears and embrace his responsibilities. This dynamic illustrates that effective mentorship is not merely about imparting knowledge but also about fostering emotional intelligence and resilience in the mentee. Krishna's teachings during the Bhagavad Gita extend beyond the battlefield, encouraging Arjuna to look beyond personal attachments and to view his role in the larger context of justice and moral duty, thus framing mentorship as a catalyst for personal growth and ethical decision-making. Furthermore, the Mahabharata presents other compelling examples of mentorship that highlight its multifaceted nature. The relationship between Drona and his students, particularly the Pandavas and Kauravas, illustrates how mentorship can shape character and influence the values of future leaders. Drona, as a master teacher, imparts not only martial skills but also lessons in loyalty, ethics, and the responsibilities of leadership. His guidance plays a crucial role in molding the identities of factions, impacting their decisions and ultimately contributing to the epic's tragic outcomes. This underscores the idea that mentors hold significant power in shaping the moral and ethical frameworks of their mentees, which can have far-reaching implications in both personal and societal contexts. Moreover, the mentorship dynamics in the Mahabharata also reveal the complexities involved in these relationships. Drona's favoritism towards Arjuna, for instance, creates tension and rivalry among his students, showcasing how mentorship can sometimes lead to unintended consequences when it lacks balance and impartiality. This aspect emphasizes that effective mentorship must also include fostering collaboration and healthy competition among mentees, allowing them to learn from each other while developing their unique strengths. The contrasting mentorship styles and their effects on character development are also evident in the epic's portrayal of Bhishma. As a revered elder and mentor figure, Bhishma embodies the ideals of duty and sacrifice, yet his steadfast adherence to his vows leads to personal tragedy and the suffering of those he seeks to protect. His complex relationship with his own sense of duty serves as a cautionary tale about the perils of rigid adherence to principles without consideration for evolving circumstances. This aspect of mentorship speaks to the necessity for mentors to remain adaptable and open-minded, recognizing that the world is ever-changing and that mentorship must evolve accordingly. Furthermore, mentorship in the Mahabharata extends beyond individual relationships to encompass broader themes of collective wisdom and guidance. The council of elders in the Kaurava court serves as a reminder of the importance of diverse perspectives in decision-making processes. When the counsel of figures like Vidura is disregarded in favor of Duryodhana's ambitions, the consequences are catastrophic, illustrating the critical need for inclusive mentorship that values the insights of those with different experiences and viewpoints. This dynamic highlights the importance of fostering a culture of mentorship within organizations and communities, where diverse voices are heard and respected, ultimately leading to more balanced and ethical decisions. In contemporary contexts, the lessons derived from the Mahabharata regarding mentorship remain highly relevant. In professional settings, mentorship is increasingly recognized as a key driver of individual and organizational success. Effective mentorship can help individuals navigate career challenges, develop leadership skills, and foster a sense of belonging and empowerment. The qualities exemplified by Krishna and other mentors in the Mahabharata—empathy, wisdom, adaptability, and moral integrity—are essential for contemporary mentors aiming to guide others through complex landscapes of personal and professional development. Additionally, the Mahabharata serves as a reminder that mentorship should be a reciprocal relationship. Just as Krishna offers guidance to Arjuna, effective mentorship also involves mentees actively engaging with their mentors, seeking feedback, and contributing to the relationship through their own insights and experiences. This reciprocity enhances the learning experience and fosters a sense of collaboration that can lead to more meaningful outcomes. Moreover, the epic emphasizes the importance of mentorship in fostering resilience and adaptability in the face of challenges. The trials faced by characters like Arjuna and the Pandavas underscore the necessity of having a mentor who not only imparts knowledge but also instills the confidence to confront adversity head-on. In today's fast-paced and often uncertain world, the ability to adapt and persevere is crucial, making mentorship an invaluable resource for individuals seeking to navigate their paths effectively. In conclusion, the importance of mentorship in the Mahabharata is woven throughout its narrative, highlighting how guidance and wisdom play a pivotal role in shaping characters, influencing ethical decision-making, and navigating complex relationships. Through the examples of Krishna, Drona, and Bhishma, the epic illustrates the multifaceted nature of mentorship and the profound impact it can have on personal and collective destinies. As we reflect on the lessons from the Mahabharata, it becomes evident that mentorship remains a timeless and essential aspect of personal and professional growth, fostering resilience, ethical leadership, and the pursuit of justice in an ever-evolving world. By embracing the qualities exemplified by the mentors in the Mahabharata, contemporary individuals can create impactful mentorship relationships that empower others, fostering a culture of learning and ethical integrity that resonates across generations.

How Krishna symbolizes the ideal mentor for leaders

Krishna's role in the Mahabharata as an ideal mentor for leaders is multifaceted and deeply influential, encapsulating the qualities of wisdom, compassion, strategic thinking, and moral integrity. His character serves as a guiding force for the Pandavas, particularly Arjuna, during pivotal moments of crisis, and his teachings extend far beyond the battlefield, addressing fundamental issues of duty, righteousness, and the complexities of human relationships. Krishna's mentorship begins in earnest during the great Kurukshetra War when Arjuna finds himself paralyzed by doubt and moral confusion about fighting against his own kin. This moment of existential crisis highlights the essential role of mentorship in leadership; just as Krishna steps in to provide guidance, leaders often encounter situations where they require counsel to navigate ethical dilemmas and personal conflicts. Krishna's approach to mentorship is characterized by a deep understanding of Arjuna's psyche, demonstrating emotional intelligence and empathy—qualities that are indispensable for effective leaders. Instead of merely instructing Arjuna on military tactics, Krishna engages him in a philosophical discourse that delves into the nature of dharma, or duty. He challenges Arjuna to rise above his attachments and fears, framing the battle as not just a personal struggle but as a necessary fight for justice and righteousness. This Socratic method of questioning encourages Arjuna to reflect deeply on his values and responsibilities, showcasing how effective mentors empower their mentees to arrive at their own conclusions, thereby fostering independent thought and moral clarity. Furthermore, Krishna's teachings in the Bhagavad Gita serve as a comprehensive guide for ethical leadership. His emphasis on the importance of acting in accordance with one's dharma—regardless of personal stakes or emotional turmoil—resonates with the challenges faced by leaders in contemporary contexts. Leaders are often tasked with making difficult decisions that require a balance between personal values and organizational goals, and Krishna's guidance underscores the need for leaders to maintain their ethical compass even amidst adversity. He emphasizes that true leadership entails not just the pursuit of success but the commitment to righteousness, integrity, and the welfare of others, aligning closely with the idea of servant leadership. Krishna also embodies the qualities of strategic thinking and adaptability—essential traits for effective mentorship. Throughout the Mahabharata, he demonstrates an exceptional ability to read situations, foresee potential outcomes, and devise strategies that align with the greater good. His diplomatic interventions, such as attempting to negotiate peace between the Pandavas and Kauravas, illustrate his foresight and understanding of the political landscape. When those efforts fail, Krishna shifts his focus to preparing the Pandavas for war, employing a multifaceted approach that includes both direct military strategies and moral encouragement. This adaptability is crucial for leaders today, as they navigate rapidly changing environments where flexibility and strategic foresight are paramount. The ability to pivot and adjust strategies based on evolving circumstances is a hallmark of effective leadership, and Krishna's mentorship exemplifies this principle. Additionally, Krishna's role as a mentor extends beyond individual relationships to encompass broader themes of community and collaboration. He emphasizes the importance of unity among the Pandavas, encouraging them to work together harmoniously despite their individual differences. This collaborative spirit is vital for leaders in any context, as effective teamwork and collective effort often lead to better outcomes than individual pursuits. Krishna's guidance fosters a sense of camaraderie and mutual support among the Pandavas, reinforcing the notion that leadership is not solely about personal glory but about uplifting others and fostering a shared vision. Moreover, Krishna's mentorship illustrates the significance of emotional resilience in leadership. Throughout the Mahabharata, he faces numerous challenges, including the moral decay surrounding him, the impending war, and the emotional turmoil of his friends and allies. Yet, he remains a steadfast source of support, embodying the qualities of calmness, rationality, and unwavering commitment to his principles. This resilience is a critical lesson for leaders, who often encounter setbacks, criticism, and moral dilemmas that can test their resolve. By maintaining a clear vision and unwavering commitment to their values, leaders can inspire confidence and loyalty among their followers, even in the face of adversity. Krishna's mentorship also emphasizes the importance of ethical decision-making and accountability. He instills in Arjuna the understanding that leadership comes with a profound responsibility to uphold justice and moral values. Krishna's insistence on righteousness serves as a reminder that leaders must not only focus on achieving goals but also consider the ethical implications of their actions. This lesson is particularly relevant in contemporary leadership contexts, where ethical lapses can lead to significant consequences for organizations and society at large. Leaders who emulate Krishna's commitment to ethical behavior can build trust and integrity within their teams, fostering a culture that prioritizes accountability and ethical practices. Furthermore, Krishna's relationship with the Pandavas highlights the mentor's role in nurturing potential and fostering growth. He recognizes Arjuna's unique strengths and encourages him to harness them, while also helping him confront his weaknesses and fears. This nurturing approach is vital for effective mentorship; leaders must recognize and cultivate the potential within their teams, providing them with the support and guidance needed to thrive. By fostering a growth-oriented environment, leaders can empower their team members to reach their full potential, enhancing overall organizational effectiveness. In addition to nurturing individual potential, Krishna also exemplifies the importance of vision in leadership. His strategic foresight and understanding of the larger picture enable him to guide the Pandavas toward their ultimate victory. He articulates a clear vision of what is right and just, inspiring his followers to align their actions with that vision. This aspect of mentorship is crucial for contemporary leaders, who must articulate a compelling vision that resonates with their teams and stakeholders. A clear and inspiring vision can motivate individuals to work collaboratively toward shared goals, driving organizational success. Krishna's ability to balance wisdom, empathy, and strategic thinking positions him as the ideal mentor for leaders navigating complex challenges. His multifaceted approach to mentorship serves as a model for contemporary leadership, emphasizing the need for emotional intelligence, ethical decision-making, and strategic adaptability. By embodying these qualities, leaders can cultivate environments that foster collaboration, resilience, and accountability, ultimately leading to more effective and ethical governance. Furthermore, the lessons derived from Krishna's mentorship extend beyond individual leaders to organizations as a whole. Institutions that prioritize mentorship, ethical leadership, and a commitment to collective well-being are better equipped to navigate the complexities of today's world. The emphasis on collaboration and community-building, as exemplified by Krishna, underscores the importance of creating inclusive environments where diverse voices are heard and respected. In this way, Krishna's legacy as an ideal mentor transcends the pages of the Mahabharata, offering timeless insights into the nature of effective leadership and mentorship. As leaders continue to face challenges in an ever-evolving landscape, the principles exemplified by Krishna remain relevant, urging contemporary leaders to embrace the values of wisdom, empathy, and moral integrity. By doing so, they can cultivate not only their own leadership potential but also empower those around them, fostering a culture of growth, ethical behavior, and collective success. In conclusion, Krishna's role as the ideal mentor for leaders in the Mahabharata is characterized by his profound wisdom, strategic thinking, and unwavering commitment to ethical principles. His mentorship transcends individual relationships, highlighting the importance of collaboration, emotional resilience, and ethical decision-making in effective leadership. As contemporary leaders draw inspiration from Krishna's teachings, they are reminded of the enduring value of mentorship in shaping not only their own paths but also the trajectories of those they lead. By embodying the qualities exemplified by Krishna, leaders can navigate the complexities of modern challenges while fostering a culture of integrity, accountability, and collective growth, ensuring that their legacies resonate far beyond their immediate circumstances.

Building Effective Advisory Boards

Building effective advisory boards can be illuminated through the insights gained from the Mahabharata, particularly by examining the intricate relationships and dynamics among its characters. An advisory board plays a crucial role in guiding leaders through complex decisions, providing diverse perspectives, and ensuring that ethical considerations are woven into the fabric of governance. The Mahabharata showcases various characters whose wisdom and counsel significantly impact the course of events, highlighting the qualities necessary for an effective advisory board. One of the most compelling examples is the council of elders in the Kaurava court, which illustrates the potential for both constructive and destructive outcomes based on the quality of advice given and heeded. The presence of wise figures like Bhishma and Vidura underscores the importance of experience and moral integrity in an advisory capacity. Bhishma, with his profound sense of duty and commitment to righteousness, embodies the ideals of loyalty and sacrifice. However, his reluctance to confront Duryodhana's misguided ambitions exemplifies a critical lesson for modern advisory boards: the necessity of fostering open dialogue and encouraging diverse opinions to avoid blind loyalty to a singular vision. An effective advisory board must cultivate an environment where differing perspectives are welcomed, enabling leaders to make informed decisions that account for various viewpoints. Vidura, on the other hand, represents the voice of reason and ethical judgment. His ability to offer sound counsel, grounded in wisdom and moral clarity, emphasizes the value of having advisors who prioritize ethical considerations over personal loyalties. His character illustrates that an effective advisory board should consist of individuals who not only possess expertise but also demonstrate a commitment to integrity and justice. The dynamics within the Kaurava court serve as a cautionary tale about the consequences of ignoring wise counsel; the failure to heed Vidura's warnings ultimately leads to devastating outcomes for the Kauravas. This emphasizes the importance of creating a culture within advisory boards where dissenting opinions can be expressed without fear of repercussions, fostering a robust decision-making process that incorporates diverse insights. Moreover, Krishna's role as an advisor to the Pandavas further illustrates the significance of mentorship and strategic guidance in leadership. Krishna's multifaceted approach combines practical strategies with profound philosophical insights, demonstrating the need for advisory boards to be composed of individuals who can offer both tactical and ethical guidance. His ability to read situations, foresee potential outcomes, and provide counsel grounded in ethical principles exemplifies the qualities that leaders should seek in their advisors. Effective advisory boards must include members who can navigate the complexities of both strategy and morality, ensuring that decisions align with broader organizational values and objectives. Furthermore, the Mahabharata highlights the importance of emotional intelligence in advisory roles. Characters like Arjuna, who often grapple with internal conflicts and moral dilemmas, benefit immensely from advisors who can empathize with their struggles and provide support. An effective advisory board should not only focus on technical expertise but also prioritize members who possess emotional intelligence, enabling them to understand and address the psychological dimensions of decision-making. This aspect is particularly relevant in today's corporate landscape, where leaders face challenges that require sensitivity to the emotional and social dynamics within their teams. Building an effective advisory board also involves recognizing the need for diversity—both in expertise and background. The varying perspectives represented in the Mahabharata, from the strategic insights of Krishna to the moral clarity of Vidura, highlight the value of diverse voices in shaping comprehensive solutions. Advisory boards should strive to include individuals with different experiences, skills, and viewpoints, fostering innovation and creativity while minimizing groupthink. This diversity can enhance the board's ability to address complex challenges and adapt to changing circumstances, ultimately leading to more effective governance. Additionally, the relationship dynamics within the Mahabharata underscore the importance of trust and mutual respect among advisory board members. The effective functioning of an advisory board relies on the ability of its members to collaborate and communicate openly. The bond between Krishna and the Pandavas exemplifies this trust; Krishna's unwavering support and guidance empower the Pandavas to embrace their destinies with confidence. Creating an environment where board members feel valued and respected fosters collaboration and encourages honest discussions, enabling leaders to draw on the full range of insights and expertise available. In conclusion, the lessons drawn from the Mahabharata provide a rich framework for building effective advisory boards. By emphasizing the importance of ethical guidance, diverse perspectives, emotional intelligence, and mutual respect, leaders can cultivate advisory boards that enhance their decision-making processes and contribute to more effective governance. The epic serves as a reminder that the quality of advice and the dynamics within advisory boards can profoundly impact the trajectory of leadership and organizational success. As contemporary leaders navigate the complexities of their roles, the insights gleaned from the Mahabharata can help shape advisory boards that not only support strategic objectives but also uphold the values of integrity and ethical responsibility.

Corporate governance models informed by the Mahabharata

Corporate governance models can draw profound insights from the Mahabharata, a text that intricately explores the principles of leadership, ethics, and the complexities of human relationships. The epic presents various characters whose decisions and actions illuminate key aspects of effective governance, highlighting the importance of moral integrity, accountability, and strategic thinking in organizational structures. One of the most salient features of governance depicted in the Mahabharata is the concept of dharma, or duty, which serves as a guiding principle for leaders in their decision-making processes. Characters such as Krishna and the Pandavas exemplify how adherence to ethical standards and a commitment to righteousness can shape successful governance. Krishna, as a mentor and advisor, underscores the necessity for leaders to align their actions with ethical values, emphasizing that true leadership is not merely about achieving success but also about fostering justice and welfare for all stakeholders. This principle can be translated into corporate governance by ensuring that organizations prioritize ethical considerations alongside financial objectives, thereby creating a culture of integrity that permeates all levels of operation. Moreover, the relationships among the characters in the Mahabharata highlight the importance of accountability and transparency in governance. The Kaurava court serves as a cautionary tale about the consequences of poor leadership and the lack of accountability, where figures like Duryodhana and Shakuni pursue personal ambitions without regard for ethical implications or the well-being of others. This dynamic illustrates the necessity for corporations to establish robust accountability mechanisms that promote transparency and ensure that leaders are held responsible for their actions. A corporate governance model informed by the Mahabharata would thus include clear guidelines for ethical behavior and accountability, fostering an environment where leaders are answerable to both their teams and stakeholders. Furthermore, the Mahabharata emphasizes the importance of inclusivity and diverse perspectives in decision-making. The contrasting approaches of characters like Vidura and Bhishma demonstrate how varying viewpoints can enrich discussions and lead to more informed decisions. This principle can be applied to corporate governance by advocating for diverse boards and advisory committees that include individuals from different backgrounds and expertise, ensuring that a wide range of perspectives is considered in strategic decisions. Inclusivity can enhance creativity and innovation within organizations, allowing them to adapt more effectively to changing environments and stakeholder needs. Additionally, the concept of collaboration and teamwork is prominent in the Mahabharata, particularly in the relationships among the Pandavas. Their ability to unite despite individual differences is a powerful lesson for corporate governance. Organizations that promote collaboration and teamwork among their leaders and employees are likely to foster a culture of mutual support and shared responsibility, ultimately leading to improved performance and employee satisfaction. Creating structures that encourage teamwork, open communication, and shared decision-making can significantly enhance organizational effectiveness and adaptability. The Mahabharata also underscores the necessity of strategic foresight in governance. Krishna's role as a strategist, guiding the Pandavas through complex dilemmas, highlights the need for leaders to possess a vision that extends beyond immediate challenges. Corporate governance models should thus incorporate long-term strategic planning, ensuring that organizations are not only reactive to current issues but also proactive in anticipating future trends and challenges. This forward-thinking approach enables organizations to navigate uncertainties effectively and position themselves advantageously in their respective markets. In conclusion, the corporate governance models informed by the Mahabharata can provide a rich framework for fostering ethical leadership, accountability, inclusivity, and strategic foresight within organizations. By embedding the principles derived from the epic into their governance structures, corporations can cultivate environments that prioritize integrity and ethical responsibility while promoting collaboration and innovation. The lessons learned from the Mahabharata are timeless and can serve as invaluable guides for contemporary organizations striving to navigate the complexities of the modern business landscape, ultimately leading to sustainable success and the well-being of all stakeholders involved.

CHAPTER SIX

❦

Team Game

Team Dynamics - The Pandavas' Brotherhood

The dynamics of team relationships are vividly illustrated in the Mahabharata through the bond of brotherhood among the Pandavas, showcasing how collaboration, mutual respect, and shared values can significantly influence group cohesion and effectiveness. The Pandavas—Yudhishthira, Bhima, Arjuna, Nakula, and Sahadeva—represent an exemplary model of teamwork rooted in their unwavering loyalty to one another, a commitment to a shared purpose, and a collective adherence to dharma, or duty. Their journey begins in adversity, with the brothers facing numerous challenges from the Kauravas, their cousins, which ultimately strengthens their bond. This initial struggle for recognition and rightful claim to their kingdom cultivates a sense of unity and purpose among them, illustrating that shared challenges can forge strong relationships and enhance teamwork. Each brother brings unique strengths to the group: Yudhishthira's wisdom and adherence to truth, Bhima's immense physical strength, Arjuna's unparalleled archery skills, and the collective knowledge of Nakula and Sahadeva in horsemanship and herbal medicine. This diversity in skills not only enhances their overall effectiveness but also fosters an environment where each brother's contributions are valued and respected. Their ability to leverage each other's strengths illustrates the importance of recognizing and appreciating the unique talents within a team, promoting a culture of collaboration rather than competition.

Besides, Mahabharata demonstrates that effective team dynamics also rely on open communication and conflict resolution. Despite their strong bond, the Pandavas experience internal conflicts and disagreements, particularly evident in the differing perspectives on leadership and strategy. However, they navigate these conflicts through respectful dialogue and by seeking consensus, which reinforces their unity and strengthens their decision-making processes. This aspect of their relationship highlights the importance of maintaining open lines of communication within teams, enabling members to express differing opinions while working toward common goals. The ability to engage in constructive conflict is essential for any effective team, as it fosters innovation and ensures that all voices are heard. The presence of Krishna as a mentor and advisor further enriches the Pandavas' teamwork. His guidance provides them with not only strategic insights but also moral support, reinforcing the significance of external mentorship in enhancing team dynamics. Krishna's ability to navigate complex situations and provide counsel underscores the importance of seeking advice and building networks of support that can help teams thrive. His role illustrates how an external perspective can bring clarity and facilitate decision-making, reinforcing the idea that effective teams are open to external insights while remaining grounded in their core values.

In addition, the Mahabharata emphasizes the role of trust and loyalty in the Pandavas' brotherhood. Their commitment to one another is unwavering, even in the face of betrayal from their cousins, the Kauravas. This deep-seated trust fosters a safe environment where the brothers can rely on each other during critical moments, such as during the exile and the climactic battle of Kurukshetra. Their loyalty not only enhances their ability to work together but also instills confidence in their collective mission, illustrating that trust is a cornerstone of effective teamwork. The Mahabharata also teaches that team dynamics can be influenced by external circumstances, such as the political landscape and familial obligations. The Pandavas navigate these challenges with resilience, learning to adapt their strategies based on changing conditions while maintaining their core principles. This adaptability is crucial for any team facing external pressures, emphasizing the importance of remaining flexible and responsive to shifts in context while staying true to shared values. In conclusion, the brotherhood of the Pandavas in the Mahabharata serves as a powerful example of effective team dynamics. Their journey highlights the significance of collaboration, open communication, trust, and adaptability in fostering strong relationships and achieving common goals. By leveraging their diverse strengths, navigating conflicts with respect, and maintaining a commitment to shared values, the Pandavas exemplify the qualities that are essential for any successful team. Their story offers timeless lessons for contemporary organizations, emphasizing the importance of cultivating cohesive teams that can navigate challenges and strive for collective success in an ever-evolving landscape.

Collaboration and Teamwork

Collaboration and teamwork are central themes in the Mahabharata, epitomized by the relationships and interactions among its characters, particularly the Pandavas. The epic vividly illustrates how effective collaboration can lead to success in the face of immense challenges, emphasizing the importance of unity, mutual respect, and shared objectives. The Pandavas, five brothers who represent the protagonists of the epic, demonstrate a remarkable ability to work together despite their individual differences, showcasing the power of teamwork in achieving a common goal. Their journey begins with adversity, marked by the usurpation of their kingdom by their cousins, the Kauravas. This initial conflict not only serves as a catalyst for their collaboration but also highlights the necessity of working together to reclaim their rightful place. The bond formed through shared struggles is a testament to how collaboration often flourishes in the face of adversity, allowing individuals to set aside personal differences for a greater purpose.

The diverse strengths of each Pandava contribute to the overall effectiveness of their team. Yudhishthira, the eldest brother, embodies wisdom and moral integrity, guiding the group with his ethical compass. His commitment to truth and justice serves as the foundation of their collective mission. Bhima, known for his immense physical strength, complements Yudhishthira's qualities with his prowess in battle, providing the necessary muscle in their quest. Arjuna, the skilled archer, represents strategic thinking and tactical prowess, bringing a wealth of experience to the battlefield. The younger brothers, Nakula and Sahadeva, contribute their own unique skills in horsemanship and knowledge of herbs, rounding out the team's capabilities. This diversity is crucial in fostering effective collaboration; by leveraging their distinct strengths, the Pandavas can tackle challenges that would be insurmountable for any one of them alone. The Mahabharata teaches that effective teams are built on the recognition and appreciation of individual contributions, creating an environment where each member feels valued and empowered. The epic emphasizes the importance of communication in fostering collaboration. The Pandavas engage in open dialogues, discussing their strategies and listening to one another's perspectives. Even in moments of disagreement, they prioritize respectful communication, allowing for constructive conflict resolution. This practice of engaging in dialogue illustrates that collaboration is not merely about harmony but also about addressing differing viewpoints to arrive at the best possible solutions. For instance, during their exile, the brothers must strategize together to survive and plan their eventual return to reclaim their kingdom. Their discussions highlight how effective communication can enhance decision-making processes and foster a sense of unity, even in challenging circumstances.

Krishna's role as a mentor further enriches the theme of collaboration and teamwork in the Mahabharata. He acts as a facilitator for the Pandavas, providing guidance and support while encouraging them to leverage their strengths collectively. His strategic insights during the Kurukshetra War highlight the necessity of external collaboration; he teaches the Pandavas to trust one another and work together in harmony, reinforcing the idea that successful teams often benefit from the guidance of a wise leader or mentor. Krishna's multifaceted approach to collaboration exemplifies how effective leadership can enhance teamwork, fostering an environment where individuals feel supported and motivated to contribute to the group's success.

The Mahabharata also explores the dynamics of teamwork in relation to the challenges posed by external forces. The Kauravas, representing not only a familial rivalry but also a formidable political opponent, embody the obstacles that teams must navigate. The conflicts between the Pandavas and Kauravas are not merely personal but symbolize larger ethical and moral dilemmas. The Pandavas' ability to unite against a common enemy illustrates how collaboration can transform adversity into an opportunity for growth and solidarity. In many ways, their conflict with the Kauravas serves as a crucible for their teamwork, forcing them to confront their individual weaknesses and learn to rely on one another's strengths. This narrative arc emphasizes that effective collaboration often arises from facing external challenges, enabling teams to develop resilience and adaptability in the process.

Furthermore, the role of mentorship and guidance within teams is exemplified by the character of Drona, the martial teacher of both the Pandavas and Kauravas. His relationship with his students illustrates the complexities of mentorship in collaborative settings. While Drona initially seeks to nurture both groups, the conflict between the Pandavas and Kauravas ultimately complicates his role. This dynamic serves as a reminder that effective collaboration is not solely dependent on individual contributions but also on the ability to navigate relationships and uphold shared values, even when personal loyalties are tested. The moral dilemmas faced by characters like Drona underscore the importance of ethical leadership and the need for teams to maintain a focus on their collective mission, even amid personal conflicts.

The theme of collaboration is further highlighted in the context of the broader alliances formed throughout the epic. The Pandavas actively seek allies to strengthen their position against the Kauravas, demonstrating the significance of external partnerships in achieving shared goals. Their alliances with figures such as Krishna, Bhishma, and other kings showcase how collaboration extends beyond the immediate team and emphasizes the importance of building networks of support. This aspect of teamwork is particularly relevant in contemporary organizational contexts, where collaboration across different sectors and stakeholders is often essential for achieving comprehensive solutions to complex problems. The Mahabharata teaches that effective teams recognize the value of collaboration not just within their immediate group but also with external partners, fostering a sense of community and shared purpose.

The Mahabharata also offers rich insights into the nature of collaboration and teamwork, as exemplified by the bond of brotherhood among the Pandavas. Their journey illustrates the importance of leveraging diverse strengths, maintaining open communication, and navigating external challenges through collective effort. The epic emphasizes that effective collaboration flourishes in the face of adversity, allowing teams to harness their collective potential in pursuit of shared goals. By fostering an environment of trust, respect, and ethical commitment, the Pandavas exemplify the qualities necessary for successful teamwork. The lessons derived from their experiences resonate in contemporary contexts, urging organizations and leaders to prioritize collaboration and teamwork as essential components of effective governance and success. Ultimately, the Mahabharata serves as a timeless reminder of the transformative power of collaboration in achieving greatness, both individually and collectively.

Dynamics of the Pandavas and their unified efforts

The dynamics of the Pandavas in the Mahabharata illustrate a profound narrative of unity, resilience, and collaborative strength in the face of adversity. As the central protagonists of the epic, the five brothers—Yudhishthira, Bhima, Arjuna, Nakula, and Sahadeva—embody the essence of teamwork, loyalty, and the importance of shared purpose, which ultimately shape their journey and define their character. Their relationship is not merely one of sibling camaraderie; it reflects a deep-seated commitment to a collective mission that transcends individual ambitions. This unity is forged through their early struggles, particularly the injustices they face at the hands of their cousins, the Kauravas, which serves as a catalyst for their collaboration and determination to reclaim their rightful place.

At the heart of the Pandavas' dynamics is their diverse set of skills and strengths. Yudhishthira, the eldest, is characterized by his unwavering adherence to dharma (righteousness) and truth, serving as the moral compass of the group. His leadership is marked by wisdom and a deep sense of justice, guiding his brothers through difficult decisions. Bhima, with his extraordinary physical strength and fierce determination, complements Yudhishthira's qualities by providing the muscle needed in battles and challenges. Arjuna, the master archer, brings not only his combat skills but also strategic insight, often serving as the tactical leader during warfare. Nakula and Sahadeva, while often in the background, contribute their expertise in horsemanship and healing, showcasing the importance of diverse talents in achieving collective goals. This diversity is a crucial element in their dynamic, allowing them to tackle challenges from multiple angles and leverage each other's strengths effectively.

The bond among the Pandavas is further strengthened by their shared experiences and the trials they endure together. Their exile, a significant turning point in the narrative, serves as a crucible for their unity. Stripped of their kingdom and forced into the wilderness, the brothers face numerous hardships that test their resilience. Instead of succumbing to despair, they find strength in one another, reinforcing their commitment to reclaiming their rightful place. This period of hardship fosters a profound sense of camaraderie, as they learn to rely on each other for emotional and physical support. The lessons learned during their exile become foundational to their future successes, emphasizing that adversity can serve as a powerful unifying force.

The role of communication in the Pandavas' dynamics cannot be overstated. Their ability to engage in open dialogue is crucial to their decision-making processes. Conflicts and disagreements arise, as seen in instances where differing opinions emerge regarding strategies or approaches to challenges. However, the Pandavas navigate these differences through respectful discourse, valuing each brother's perspective. This practice of engaging in constructive conversations fosters an environment of trust and mutual respect, allowing them to reach consensus even in the face of conflicting views. This dynamic is particularly evident in the context of their preparations for the Kurukshetra War, where strategic discussions and collaboration become essential for formulating effective plans against the formidable Kaurava forces. Krishna's mentorship further enriches the Pandavas' collaborative efforts. As their charioteer and advisor, Krishna provides invaluable guidance, helping the brothers navigate complex moral dilemmas and strategic choices. His influence emphasizes the importance of external support in enhancing team dynamics. Krishna's wisdom and strategic foresight encourage the Pandavas to harness their individual strengths and work together harmoniously. His presence serves as a reminder that effective teamwork often benefits from mentorship and the guidance of experienced leaders, who can offer insights that enhance collective efforts.

The dynamics of the Pandavas also highlight the concept of shared responsibility. Each brother recognizes their role within the group, contributing to a sense of collective ownership over their mission. This shared responsibility is particularly evident during the Kurukshetra War, where each brother plays a critical role in their strategy and execution. Yudhishthira's leadership and ethical grounding, Bhima's formidable strength, Arjuna's archery skills, and Nakula and Sahadeva's contributions in various capacities underscore the importance of everyone's involvement. Their unified efforts during this climactic battle illustrate how collaboration can amplify their effectiveness and ultimately lead to triumph against overwhelming odds. The emotional bonds between the brothers also play a significant role in their dynamics. The shared sense of loss, particularly following the death of their father, Pandu, creates a deeper emotional connection that strengthens their unity. This bond extends to their mutual respect and admiration for one another, allowing them to support each other through personal struggles and challenges. For instance, Bhima's fierce loyalty to his brothers and Arjuna's deep sense of responsibility toward his family highlight the emotional depth of their relationships, reinforcing the idea that strong emotional ties can enhance team dynamics and foster resilience.

Furthermore, the challenges posed by the Kauravas serve as a backdrop against which the Pandavas' unity is tested and ultimately solidified. The Kauravas, led by Duryodhana, represent not only a familial rivalry but also the moral and ethical dilemmas that the Pandavas must navigate. The conflict becomes a powerful motivator for their unified efforts, as they recognize the need to stand together against injustice and oppression. This external threat catalyzes their collaboration, transforming their shared mission into a battle for righteousness and dharma. The dynamics of the Pandavas in the Mahabharata exemplify the power of collaboration and unity in overcoming adversity. Their diverse strengths, open communication, shared experiences, and mutual support create a cohesive and effective team capable of navigating the complexities of their journey. The bond forged through trials and tribulations serves as a powerful reminder of the importance of collaboration in achieving common goals. The lessons learned from the Pandavas' unified efforts resonate in contemporary contexts, emphasizing that teamwork, trust, and shared responsibility are essential for success in any endeavor. Ultimately, the Mahabharata offers timeless insights into the dynamics of collaboration, illustrating how unity can lead to triumph even in the face of overwhelming challenges.

Modern Business Teams

The Mahabharata offers rich insights into the dynamics of teamwork, which are highly relevant to modern business environments. The epic's portrayal of the Pandavas illustrates essential principles of collaboration, diversity, and leadership that can guide contemporary organizations in fostering effective teams. At its core, the Mahabharata emphasizes the importance of unity in purpose, shared values, and leveraging individual strengths to achieve common goals—all critical components of successful modern business teams.

One of the most striking aspects of the Pandavas' teamwork is their ability to blend diverse skills and perspectives. Each brother brings unique attributes to the table: Yudhishthira's wisdom and moral integrity, Bhima's immense physical strength, Arjuna's unmatched archery and strategic thinking, and Nakula and Sahadeva's expertise in horsemanship and healing. This diversity mirrors the modern emphasis on assembling teams with varied skill sets and backgrounds, recognizing that a blend of talents leads to more innovative solutions and better decision-making. In contemporary business, teams that encompass diverse experiences and viewpoints are better equipped to tackle complex challenges and adapt to rapidly changing markets.

The importance of effective communication is another critical lesson from the Mahabharata that resonates in today's corporate landscape. The Pandavas exemplify how open dialogue and respectful discourse can resolve conflicts and enhance collaboration. When faced with disagreements, they engage in discussions that allow each member to express their views, ultimately arriving at a consensus. In modern business, fostering an environment where team members feel safe to voice their opinions and ideas is essential for cultivating creativity and innovation. Companies that prioritize open communication are more likely to create a culture of trust, where employees feel valued and empowered to contribute to the team's success.

Krishna's role as a mentor and advisor to the Pandavas underscores the significance of leadership and guidance in team dynamics. His strategic insights and moral support empower the brothers to navigate complex situations, highlighting the need for leaders who can facilitate collaboration and inspire their teams. In contemporary business, effective leaders not only provide direction but also serve as mentors, helping team members develop their skills and navigate challenges. This leadership style fosters a sense of loyalty and commitment, creating a cohesive team that is motivated to achieve its objectives.

Moreover, the concept of shared responsibility is integral to the Pandavas' success and is a crucial principle for modern business teams. Each brother recognizes and embraces their individual roles while working collectively toward their shared goal of reclaiming their kingdom. This sense of accountability extends beyond personal contributions to encompass the success of the team as a whole. In today's workplace, establishing clear roles and responsibilities while promoting a culture of collective ownership can enhance team performance. When team members feel accountable not only for their tasks but also for supporting their colleagues, it fosters collaboration and strengthens the group's overall effectiveness.

The trials and tribulations faced by the Pandavas, particularly during their exile, serve as a testament to the resilience that effective teams can cultivate. Adversity often brings teams closer together, fostering a sense of camaraderie and shared purpose. In modern business, challenges such as market fluctuations, technological disruptions, or internal conflicts can act as catalysts for team growth. By facing obstacles together, teams can build trust and enhance their problem-solving capabilities, turning potential setbacks into opportunities for learning and development. Also, the external conflict with the Kauravas highlights the significance of having a common enemy or goal, which can galvanize a team's efforts. For the Pandavas, the battle against injustice serves as a unifying force, motivating them to collaborate effectively. In the context of modern business, having a shared vision or mission can inspire teams to rally together, aligning their efforts toward achieving collective objectives. Organizations that articulate a clear mission and involve their teams in the vision-setting process are likely to foster a strong sense of unity and purpose among their employees.

The Mahabharata also illustrates the necessity of adaptability in teamwork. The Pandavas often face unforeseen challenges that require them to adjust their strategies and tactics. Their ability to remain flexible and responsive to changing circumstances is a vital lesson for modern business teams, particularly in today's fast-paced environment where change is the only constant. Teams that can pivot quickly in response to new information or market conditions are better positioned to thrive and succeed. The lessons derived from the dynamics of the Pandavas in the Mahabharata offer valuable insights for modern business teams. By embracing diversity, fostering open communication, and promoting shared responsibility, organizations can cultivate effective teams capable of navigating the complexities of contemporary challenges. The epic underscores the importance of mentorship, resilience, and adaptability—qualities that are essential for success in today's rapidly evolving business landscape. Ultimately, the principles illustrated by the Pandavas remind us that effective teamwork is not just a strategy for achieving goals; it is a powerful catalyst for innovation, growth, and sustained success.

Strategies for fostering teamwork and collaboration in organizations

Fostering teamwork and collaboration in organizations is essential for achieving shared goals and driving innovation. The Mahabharata offers timeless lessons on collaboration through the dynamics of the Pandavas, whose strong bonds and unified efforts exemplify effective teamwork. By drawing on the principles illustrated in this epic, modern organizations can implement strategies to enhance collaboration among their teams.

Encouraging Open Communication

One of the most significant lessons from the Mahabharata is the importance of open communication. The Pandavas engage in respectful dialogues, allowing each brother to express their thoughts and concerns. This open exchange not only resolves conflicts but also strengthens their unity. In contemporary organizations, fostering a culture of transparency encourages team members to voice their opinions without fear of reprisal. Regular check-ins, team meetings, and feedback sessions can create a safe environment for sharing ideas and addressing issues, ultimately enhancing collaboration.

Building Trust and Respect

Trust is the cornerstone of effective teamwork, as demonstrated by the unwavering loyalty among the Pandavas. Their ability to rely on one another, especially during challenging times, highlights the necessity of cultivating trust within teams. Organizations can build trust by promoting inclusivity, recognizing individual contributions, and encouraging team members to support one another. Activities that require collaboration, such as team-building exercises or cross-departmental projects, can foster relationships and enhance mutual respect, creating a more cohesive work environment.

Diversity and Inclusion

The Pandavas' unique strengths exemplify the benefits of diversity in a team. Each brother contributes different skills—Yudhishthira's wisdom, Bhima's strength, Arjuna's strategic prowess, and Nakula and Sahadeva's expertise. Organizations can harness the power of diversity by assembling teams with varied backgrounds, experiences, and perspectives. Encouraging diverse viewpoints not only fosters creativity and innovation but also leads to more comprehensive problem-solving. Creating an inclusive environment where everyone feels valued will enhance collaboration and drive better outcomes.

Defining Roles and Responsibilities

Clarity in roles is essential for effective teamwork. In the Mahabharata, each Pandava embraces their role, contributing to the team's overall success. Organizations should ensure that every team member understands their specific responsibilities and how their contributions align with the team's objectives. Clearly defined roles help reduce ambiguity, enhance accountability, and promote a sense of ownership over tasks. When individuals recognize their impact on the team's success, they are more likely to collaborate effectively and work toward common goals.

Setting Shared Goals

The Pandavas are united by their shared mission to reclaim their kingdom, which drives their collaboration. Similarly, organizations should establish clear, collective goals that inspire team members to work together. These goals should be communicated effectively, ensuring that everyone understands the organization's vision and their role in achieving it. Involving team members in the goal-setting process fosters a sense of ownership and accountability, motivating individuals to contribute their best efforts toward the shared objectives.

Fostering a Supportive Environment

The Mahabharata highlights the significance of emotional support among the Pandavas. During difficult times, they lean on one another for encouragement and strength. Modern organizations can create a supportive environment by promoting mental well-being, recognizing individual challenges, and providing resources for personal and professional development. Establishing mentorship programs, peer support networks, and wellness initiatives can help employees feel valued and supported, which in turn enhances collaboration and teamwork.

Encouraging Constructive Conflict

While collaboration thrives on harmony, constructive conflict is also essential for growth. The Pandavas navigate disagreements through respectful dialogue, using these moments to arrive at better solutions. Organizations should encourage a culture where differing viewpoints are welcomed and discussed openly. Training team members in conflict resolution techniques can help them navigate disagreements productively, transforming potential conflicts into opportunities for collaboration and innovation.

Utilizing Technology to Enhance Collaboration

In the digital age, technology plays a vital role in fostering teamwork. The Pandavas relied on strategic guidance from Krishna, which mirrors how modern tools can facilitate collaboration. Organizations should leverage collaboration platforms, project management software, and communication tools to enhance connectivity among team members. These technologies can streamline workflows, enhance information sharing, and ensure that everyone is aligned on goals and tasks, making collaboration more efficient and effective.

Recognizing and Celebrating Team Achievements

The Mahabharata showcases the importance of recognizing individual and collective efforts. Celebrating successes—whether big or small—can enhance morale and foster a sense of belonging within the team. Organizations should implement recognition programs that highlight team achievements, promote peer-to-peer recognition, and celebrate milestones. Acknowledging contributions not only motivates individuals but also strengthens team cohesion and reinforces the importance of collaboration.

Continuous Learning and Adaptability

The Pandavas' ability to adapt to changing circumstances is crucial to their success. Organizations should foster a culture of continuous learning, encouraging team members to develop new skills and embrace change. Providing opportunities for professional development, training, and cross-functional experiences can enhance collaboration by equipping employees with the tools they need to navigate challenges effectively. An adaptable team is more likely to thrive in dynamic environments and leverage collaboration to overcome obstacles.

The dynamics of the Pandavas in the Mahabharata offer valuable lessons for fostering teamwork and collaboration in modern organizations. By encouraging open communication, building trust, embracing diversity, defining roles, setting shared goals, and creating a supportive environment, organizations can cultivate a culture of collaboration that drives success. Ultimately, the principles illustrated in this epic remind us that effective teamwork is not only about achieving objectives but also about building strong relationships and fostering a sense of community among team members. Embracing these strategies can empower organizations to navigate challenges and seize opportunities through the strength of collaboration.

✿

CHAPTER SEVEN

Risk Management

The Cost of War - Assessing Risks in Business

The theme of war in the Mahabharata serves as a profound metaphor for the risks and costs associated with business decisions, illustrating that the consequences of conflict extend far beyond the immediate battlefield. The epic's central conflict—the Kurukshetra War—presents a stark portrayal of the devastating impacts of rivalry, ambition, and ethical dilemmas, paralleling the high stakes involved in contemporary business environments. Just as the Pandavas and Kauravas faced catastrophic consequences due to their pursuit of power and territory, modern organizations must assess the risks inherent in their strategic decisions, weighing potential gains against the costs of conflict. The Mahabharata emphasizes that war, while often seen as a means to resolve disputes, ultimately results in profound loss, suffering, and long-term repercussions that can undermine the very foundations of a society or an organization. In business, this translates to recognizing that aggressive competition, unethical practices, or poorly considered strategies can lead to significant financial losses, reputational damage, and a toxic corporate culture. The epic illustrates that decisions made in the heat of ambition can lead to unintended consequences, such as the alienation of allies, loss of trust among stakeholders, and the erosion of ethical standards. For instance, Duryodhana's relentless quest for power blinds him to the potential fallout of his actions, culminating in a war that devastates both his forces and the Pandavas, resulting in countless deaths and the destruction of kinship ties. This serves as a cautionary tale for businesses: a focus on short-term gains can obscure the long-term ramifications of decisions, leading to a cycle of conflict and loss. Furthermore, the Mahabharata underscores the importance of foresight and strategic planning in mitigating risks. The Pandavas, particularly through the guidance of Krishna, exemplify the need to assess the broader implications of their actions before entering the battlefield. They weigh their options, consider alliances, and recognize the moral dimensions of their choices. In the business world, this translates to the necessity of conducting thorough risk assessments, market analyses, and ethical evaluations before pursuing aggressive strategies. Organizations that fail to anticipate potential risks—be they market volatility, competitive retaliation, or shifts in consumer sentiment—risk entering conflicts that could jeopardize their sustainability. Additionally, the epic illustrates the collateral damage of war, which serves as a reminder of the indirect costs that businesses can incur. The loss of human capital, destruction of resources, and long-term psychological impacts on employees can be compared to the societal ramifications of war depicted in the Mahabharata. As the battle rages on, not only do warriors perish, but entire communities suffer, and the fabric of society is irreparably damaged. For businesses, this reflects the need to consider the human aspect of their decisions; conflicts can lead to employee disengagement, high turnover rates, and a culture of fear and mistrust. Therefore, fostering a collaborative environment and seeking peaceful resolutions to conflicts becomes paramount, aligning with the ethos of ethical leadership and responsibility that Krishna embodies throughout the epic. Moreover, the aftermath of the Kurukshetra War teaches important lessons about recovery and rebuilding. After the conflict, the surviving characters must confront the devastation left in the wake of their choices, grappling with loss and the moral weight of their actions. This serves as a powerful reminder for organizations to prepare for post-conflict recovery; businesses should have strategies in place for crisis management, reputation rebuilding, and stakeholder engagement following contentious situations. The ability to learn from past mistakes and adapt strategies accordingly is crucial in navigating the complex landscape of modern business. Ultimately, the Mahabharata illustrates that the cost of war—whether literal or metaphorical—demands a comprehensive understanding of risks, the necessity of ethical considerations, and the importance of strategic foresight. In today's business environment, organizations must cultivate a culture that prioritizes collaboration, ethical decision-making and long-term sustainability over short-term victories. By learning from the epic's insights, businesses can navigate conflicts more effectively, mitigating risks while striving for success in a competitive landscape. Thus, the lessons from the Mahabharata resonate powerfully, underscoring that the true cost of war extends far beyond immediate losses, shaping the future of individuals, organizations, and societies alike.

Understanding the Consequences of Conflict

Understanding the consequences of conflict in the Mahabharata provides profound insights into the multifaceted repercussions that arise from discord, illustrating how rivalry and war can lead to devastating outcomes that extend beyond the battlefield. The epic's central narrative—the Kurukshetra War—serves as a stark reminder of the destructive potential of unresolved conflicts, as it not only results in the loss of life but also disrupts familial bonds, erodes moral values, and leaves lasting scars on society. As the Pandavas and Kauravas engage in their fierce struggle for power, the consequences of their actions unfold dramatically, revealing that conflict often begets further conflict, creating a cycle of vengeance and despair. The death of key figures, such as Bhishma and Drona, highlights how personal loss reverberates through the community, affecting not just the immediate parties involved but also future generations. The epic illustrates that the fallout of conflict can manifest in various forms, including emotional trauma, societal disintegration, and a pervasive sense of grief that lingers long after the fighting has ceased. This understanding is crucial for contemporary contexts, as organizations facing internal or external conflicts must recognize that the implications of their disputes can have far-reaching effects on morale, culture, and reputation. Additionally, the Mahabharata emphasizes the ethical dilemmas that arise in conflict situations, showcasing characters who grapple with their choices and the moral implications of their actions. For instance, Yudhishthira's struggle with the truth and his eventual decisions reflect the weight of ethical considerations during wartime, highlighting that conflicts often compel individuals to compromise their values, leading to a loss of integrity and trust. In the realm of modern business, this serves as a cautionary tale: the drive for competitive advantage can tempt organizations to engage in unethical practices that, while seemingly beneficial in the short term, ultimately undermine their credibility and long-term success. The consequences of conflict also extend to the impact on leadership and governance. The Mahabharata portrays various leadership styles, contrasting the decisions made by wise leaders like Krishna with the reckless ambition of Duryodhana. This dichotomy illustrates how leadership during times of conflict can shape the trajectory of outcomes; effective leaders must navigate disputes thoughtfully, seeking resolutions that prioritize dialogue and understanding over aggression. In contemporary organizations, this underscores the necessity of cultivating leaders who can manage conflicts constructively, fostering a culture of collaboration rather than one marked by divisiveness. Furthermore, the epic reveals the importance of allyship and diplomacy in mitigating the consequences of conflict. The failure of the Kauravas to recognize the value of alliances leads to their isolation and eventual downfall, emphasizing that building relationships and seeking common ground can prevent conflicts from escalating into destructive confrontations. Modern organizations can learn from this by prioritizing collaboration and communication, recognizing that a cooperative approach can lead to more sustainable solutions and lessened fallout from disputes. Ultimately, the Mahabharata teaches that the consequences of conflict are not confined to immediate outcomes but extend into the moral, emotional, and social fabric of society. The reverberations of the Kurukshetra War serve as a poignant reminder that conflicts can reshape identities, alter relationships, and change the course of history. For businesses, this means that addressing conflicts proactively and ethically is not only crucial for preserving individual relationships but also for maintaining organizational health and societal impact. By understanding the far-reaching consequences of conflict as illustrated in the Mahabharata, leaders and organizations can approach disputes with greater awareness and responsibility, striving for resolutions that acknowledge the complexity of human relationships and the intricate web of consequences that conflict entails. In doing so, they can foster environments that prioritize healing, collaboration, and ethical leadership, ultimately leading to more positive outcomes in both business and society at large.

The aftermath of the Kurukshetra War and its allegories in business battles

The aftermath of the Kurukshetra War in the Mahabharata serves as a powerful allegory for the repercussions of business battles, illustrating the profound impacts that conflict can have on individuals, organizations, and society as a whole. Following the epic confrontation between the Pandavas and the Kauravas, the once-vibrant kingdom of Hastinapura lies in ruins, steeped in grief and loss, with countless lives extinguished and the social fabric irreparably altered. This somber conclusion reflects the harsh realities that can follow competitive conflicts in the business world, where aggressive rivalries and cutthroat strategies often yield significant collateral damage. Just as the Pandavas are left to grapple with the moral implications of their victory—facing the haunting specters of their fallen kin and allies—organizations that emerge triumphant from hostile business environments must confront the ethical and relational costs of their victories. The Mahabharata poignantly illustrates how the thirst for power can lead to devastating consequences, emphasizing that the spoils of victory may not outweigh the losses incurred during the struggle. In the corporate realm, this is mirrored in the aftermath of hostile takeovers, aggressive mergers, or brutal competitive tactics that, while potentially successful in achieving short-term goals, can lead to long-term reputational damage, employee disengagement, and a toxic workplace culture. The epic also highlights the importance of leadership in navigating the aftermath of conflict; Yudhishthira's ascension to the throne brings with it a heavy burden of responsibility as he seeks to restore order and rebuild a fractured society. In a business context, leaders must similarly address the fallout of their competitive actions, taking responsibility for the well-being of their employees, stakeholders, and the community. The process of recovery requires not only strategic planning but also a genuine commitment to ethical practices, transparent communication, and rebuilding trust among all parties involved. Furthermore, the allegories of the Mahabharata extend to the need for reflection and learning from past mistakes. The Pandavas, despite their victory, are deeply affected by the moral and emotional toll of the war, prompting them to reassess their values and priorities. This introspection serves as a crucial lesson for businesses: engaging in self-reflection and analyzing the consequences of one's strategies can lead to more responsible decision-making in the future. By acknowledging the complexity of human relationships and the potential for conflict to cause harm, organizations can cultivate a more compassionate approach to competition, fostering collaboration over animosity. Ultimately, the aftermath of the Kurukshetra War serves as a stark reminder that the battles fought in business—much like those in the epic—can yield significant consequences that extend beyond financial metrics. The need for reconciliation, ethical leadership, and a commitment to rebuilding trust resonates deeply in both the Mahabharata and modern business landscapes. By drawing on these lessons, organizations can navigate the complexities of competitive environments with greater awareness, striving for outcomes that prioritize ethical considerations and the well-being of all stakeholders involved, thereby transforming potential conflicts into opportunities for growth and collaboration.

Risk Management

Risk management in the context of the Mahabharata underscores the importance of foresight, strategic planning, and ethical decision-making in navigating conflicts and uncertainties. Throughout the epic, the characters frequently confront significant risks that challenge their values, alliances, and survival, serving as powerful allegories for contemporary risk management practices. One of the most notable examples is Yudhishthira's adherence to dharma, or righteousness, as he assesses the moral implications of his decisions before entering the Kurukshetra War. His commitment to ethical principles illustrates that effective risk management involves not only evaluating potential outcomes but also aligning actions with core values. Similarly, Krishna's role as a strategist and advisor to the Pandavas exemplifies the necessity of informed decision-making in the face of adversity. He carefully analyzes the strengths and weaknesses of both sides, offering guidance that enables the Pandavas to mitigate risks and capitalize on their advantages. This emphasizes the importance of gathering relevant information and seeking counsel from knowledgeable sources, a practice that is crucial in today's risk management frameworks. The epic also highlights the unpredictable nature of conflicts, as the characters must remain adaptable and responsive to changing circumstances. For instance, the shifting alliances and betrayals that occur throughout the story illustrate how unforeseen events can drastically alter the landscape of conflict, necessitating a proactive approach to risk management. In a business context, this translates to developing contingency plans and fostering a culture of agility that allows organizations to pivot quickly in response to emerging threats or opportunities. Additionally, the consequences faced by characters who disregard the importance of risk assessment serve as cautionary tales. Duryodhana's underestimation of the Pandavas' resolve and the reliance on deceitful tactics ultimately lead to his downfall, highlighting the perils of hubris and lack of strategic foresight. This aligns with the modern understanding that ignoring potential risks can lead to catastrophic outcomes. Therefore, organizations must cultivate a mindset that values comprehensive risk analysis, ethical decision-making, and collaboration in order to navigate the complexities of today's business environment. In conclusion, the lessons drawn from the Mahabharata regarding risk management emphasize that success in any endeavor—be it in war or business—requires a careful balance of ethical considerations, strategic planning, and adaptability to effectively mitigate risks and achieve sustainable outcomes.

Lessons on navigating risks and preparing for crises

The Mahabharata provides rich lessons on navigating risks and preparing for crises, emphasizing the importance of foresight, ethical decision-making, and the power of alliances in overcoming adversity. Central to the epic is the impending conflict of the Kurukshetra War, which serves as a backdrop for exploring how characters confront various risks and prepare for the consequences of their actions. One of the key lessons is the necessity of understanding the broader implications of decisions. Yudhishthira, despite his noble intentions, often grapples with the weight of his choices, illustrating those ethical considerations must guide decision-making, particularly in times of uncertainty. His commitment to dharma, or righteousness, highlights the idea that aligning actions with moral values can mitigate risks and foster trust among allies. In contemporary contexts, this underscores the importance of establishing a strong ethical framework within organizations, ensuring that decisions are not solely driven by short-term gains but also consider long-term implications for stakeholders and society at large. Furthermore, the role of Krishna as a mentor and strategist is paramount in navigating the complexities of impending conflict. His counsel to the Pandavas emphasizes the need for thorough preparation and the importance of gathering intelligence about potential threats. He advocates for strategic alliances, exemplified by the various support the Pandavas secure, including from powerful figures like Bhishma and Drona. This highlights the significance of building relationships and fostering collaboration as a means of risk mitigation; in the business world, cultivating partnerships and networks can enhance resilience and create a support system that proves invaluable during crises. The Mahabharata also teaches the value of adaptability and proactive crisis management. Characters often face unexpected challenges that force them to adjust their strategies. For instance, the Pandavas' ability to remain agile in their tactics reflects the need for businesses to develop contingency plans and be ready to pivot in response to changing circumstances. The importance of resilience is further underscored by the aftermath of the war, where the surviving characters must grapple with profound loss and rebuild their society. This serves as a powerful reminder that effective crisis management involves not only addressing immediate threats but also focusing on recovery and rebuilding in the long term. Businesses, too, must prepare for crises by establishing robust risk management frameworks that include both preventive measures and responsive strategies, ensuring they can navigate disruptions and emerge stronger. Additionally, the consequences faced by characters who underestimate risks serve as cautionary tales. Duryodhana's downfall illustrates the perils of hubris and complacency in the face of adversity; his failure to recognize the resolve of his opponents leads to catastrophic consequences. This reinforces the importance of maintaining vigilance and continually assessing the risk landscape. Organizations should adopt a proactive approach to risk assessment, regularly evaluating internal and external factors that could impact their operations. Lastly, the Mahabharata emphasizes the significance of communication during crises. The ability to convey intentions, rally support, and maintain transparency can be critical in mitigating misunderstandings and fostering solidarity among stakeholders. The Pandavas' journey showcases how clear communication and a united front can inspire confidence and resilience in times of turmoil. In summary, the lessons derived from the Mahabharata regarding navigating risks and preparing for crises highlight the need for ethical decision-making, strategic alliances, adaptability, and effective communication. By embracing these principles, organizations can enhance their resilience and preparedness, ensuring they are equipped to face uncertainties and emerge successfully from challenges, much like the Pandavas who, despite their losses, ultimately strive to restore order and justice in their realm.

CHAPTER EIGHT

Youth and Innovation

Youth and Innovation - The Role of Abhimanyu

Abhimanyu, the valiant son of Arjuna and Subhadra in the Mahabharata, embodies the themes of youth and innovation, serving as a powerful symbol of the potential for fresh perspectives and bold ideas in the face of overwhelming challenges. Despite his young age, Abhimanyu displays remarkable courage and strategic acumen, particularly during the Kurukshetra War, where he distinguishes himself by navigating the complex and formidable Chakravyuha formation. His ability to penetrate this intricate battle strategy, learned while still in the womb, exemplifies how innovative thinking and youthful enthusiasm can lead to significant breakthroughs, even in dire circumstances. Abhimanyu's approach underscores the importance of adaptability; he relies not on conventional tactics but instead draws on his unique insights and skills, demonstrating that fresh perspectives can disrupt entrenched patterns and lead to new possibilities. This is particularly relevant in today's rapidly changing business landscape, where organizations must harness the creativity and ingenuity of younger generations to stay competitive and responsive to market demands. Additionally, Abhimanyu's character illustrates the challenges faced by youth in positions of innovation. His bravery and skills, while commendable, are tragically met with overwhelming odds, revealing the harsh realities that often accompany ambitious endeavors. This serves as a poignant reminder that innovation requires not only talent and courage but also support and mentorship to thrive. The collective efforts of his elder kin, coupled with his youthful zeal, highlight the need for collaboration between generations, where the experience of seasoned leaders can complement the innovative spirit of youth. Ultimately, Abhimanyu's story emphasizes that investing in young talent and fostering an environment that encourages innovative thinking is crucial for any society or organization. By empowering the next generation to challenge norms and explore new ideas, organizations can cultivate a culture of creativity that propels them forward, much like Abhimanyu's daring actions on the battlefield, which, despite their tragic outcome, serve as a testament to the transformative power of youth and innovation in the face of adversity.

Abhimanyu's Bravery and Young Leadership

Abhimanyu's bravery and young leadership in the Mahabharata serve as a profound testament to the qualities of courage, resilience, and strategic thinking that can define effective leadership, even in the face of overwhelming odds. As the son of Arjuna and Subhadra, Abhimanyu is imbued with the valiant spirit of the Pandavas, yet he represents a unique blend of youthful enthusiasm and tactical insight that sets him apart on the battlefield of Kurukshetra. His most notable act of bravery occurs during the intense confrontation known as the Chakravyuha, a complex military formation that few could penetrate. Having learned about this intricate strategy while still in his mother's womb, Abhimanyu demonstrates not only his innate courage but also his capacity for learning and adapting, which are critical traits for any leader.

When the opportunity arises to breach the Chakravyuha, Abhimanyu steps forward with unwavering determination, fully aware of the risks involved. His decision to take on such a daunting challenge highlights a significant aspect of young leadership: the willingness to embrace risks for the greater good. Unlike some of the more seasoned warriors, who may hesitate due to fear or the burden of past experiences, Abhimanyu's youthful perspective enables him to act decisively. This characteristic reflects a common trait among younger leaders: the ability to see possibilities where others see obstacles, fostering a spirit of innovation and bold action.

However, Abhimanyu's bravery is not solely defined by his physical prowess; it also encompasses his mental fortitude and tactical acumen. As he penetrates the Chakravyuha, he exhibits strategic thinking, using his knowledge to navigate the formation and engage effectively with formidable adversaries. Yet, his isolated position also serves as a poignant reminder of the vulnerabilities that can accompany youthful leadership. Abhimanyu finds himself surrounded and ultimately outnumbered, illustrating that even the most courageous leaders require support and collaboration to thrive. His tragic fate highlights the crucial importance of mentorship and teamwork, underscoring that young leader must be integrated into a supportive framework where their talents can be maximized.

Moreover, Abhimanyu's leadership qualities resonate beyond the battlefield; they inspire those around him, rallying fellow warriors and instilling a sense of hope and courage in his comrades. His willingness to fight valiantly, even against insurmountable odds, serves as a powerful motivator, demonstrating how a leader's bravery can galvanize others to action. This aspect of his character reflects an essential principle of effective leadership: the ability to inspire and uplift others, fostering a collective resolve to confront challenges.

In contemporary contexts, Abhimanyu's example is particularly relevant as organizations increasingly recognize the value of young leaders who bring fresh perspectives and innovative ideas. His story illustrates the importance of nurturing and empowering youth within leadership roles, providing them with the mentorship and resources needed to navigate complex challenges. By creating environments that embrace youthful energy and creativity while ensuring the presence of experienced guidance, organizations can cultivate leaders who are not only brave but also effective in driving meaningful change.

Abhimanyu's bravery and young leadership encapsulate vital lessons for both ancient and modern contexts. His actions on the battlefield serve as a reminder that courage, strategic insight, and the ability to inspire others are crucial components of effective leadership. By understanding and embracing these qualities, organizations can foster a new generation of leaders capable of navigating the complexities of their environments, ultimately shaping a brighter future in the face of adversity.

Lessons on perspective from youth in shaping business futures

The Mahabharata offers profound lessons on the value of youth and their perspectives in shaping business futures, epitomized by the character of Abhimanyu, who exemplifies the boldness, creativity, and adaptability often found in young leaders. Abhimanyu's daring act of breaching the formidable Chakravyuha, despite his limited experience, highlights how fresh insights can challenge established norms and drive innovation. In the corporate world, this mirrors the necessity for organizations to embrace the ideas and enthusiasm of younger employees who, unburdened by the conventional thinking that may dominate their senior counterparts, can propose innovative solutions to complex problems. Abhimanyu's journey also underscores the importance of mentorship; while he displays remarkable bravery and strategic thinking, his isolation during the battle serves as a cautionary tale about the need for guidance and support from experienced leaders. This dynamic illustrates that for youth perspectives to truly flourish, organizations must foster an environment of collaboration where knowledge is shared across generations, enabling young leaders to thrive while benefitting from the wisdom of their elders. Furthermore, Abhimanyu's unwavering commitment to dharma—or righteousness—demonstrates that youth can bring fresh ethical perspectives that challenge outdated practices and advocate for integrity in decision-making. In today's business landscape, where corporate responsibility and ethical considerations are paramount, cultivating a culture that empowers young leaders to prioritize values can enhance organizational reputation and sustainability. Additionally, the ability of youth to inspire and motivate others is a vital lesson from the Mahabharata; Abhimanyu's courage rallies those around him, fostering unity and collective resolve, which is essential for driving teams toward shared goals. This capacity to galvanize support and enthusiasm among peers can significantly enhance team dynamics and performance in organizations. Ultimately, the Mahabharata illustrates that embracing the perspectives of youth is not merely an exercise in inclusivity but a strategic imperative for businesses seeking to navigate the complexities of modern markets. By valuing adaptability, promoting mentorship, encouraging ethical leadership, and harnessing the inspiring potential of young leaders, organizations can create a vibrant culture of innovation that propels them toward sustainable success. The lessons gleaned from Abhimanyu's character remind us that the future of any organization is intricately linked to the voices of its youth, making it crucial to cultivate environments where their ideas and insights can flourish, ultimately shaping a brighter and more resilient future for all.

Encouraging Innovation

Encouraging innovation is a vital theme in the Mahabharata, vividly illustrated through the character of Abhimanyu, whose audacious approach to the Chakravyuha represents the transformative power of creative thinking. His ability to penetrate this complex military formation, learned in the womb, highlights the importance of fresh ideas and perspectives in overcoming seemingly insurmountable challenges. In the context of business, this narrative underscores the necessity for organizations to foster an environment that values creativity and encourages individuals to think outside the box. By creating spaces where unconventional solutions are welcomed and experimentation is supported, businesses can harness the innovative spirit that youth like Abhimanyu embody. Furthermore, the epic emphasizes collaboration; Abhimanyu's actions inspire his comrades, demonstrating how collective innovation can arise when diverse talents and ideas are united. Just as Krishna serves as a mentor and guide to the Pandavas, leaders in contemporary organizations must provide the necessary support and resources for their teams to explore new concepts and challenge existing paradigms. Ultimately, the Mahabharata teaches that encouraging innovation not only drives progress but also cultivates a culture of resilience and adaptability, essential for thriving in an ever-changing landscape.

How to cultivate a culture of innovation and agility in organizations

Cultivating a culture of innovation and agility in organizations can draw valuable insights from the Mahabharata, particularly through the experiences of its characters and their interactions during times of crisis. The epic emphasizes the importance of adaptability, collaboration, and strategic thinking—essential components for fostering an innovative environment.

One of the key lessons is illustrated by Abhimanyu's courageous breach of the Chakravyuha. His ability to devise a strategy to navigate this complex military formation showcases the need for organizations to encourage creative problem-solving. Leaders can cultivate innovation by creating safe spaces for employees to experiment with new ideas, much like Abhimanyu's bold approach. This involves recognizing and rewarding initiative and risk-taking, allowing team members to learn from both successes and failures without fear of repercussion.

Additionally, the role of Krishna as a mentor and strategist emphasizes the value of guidance and collaboration in nurturing innovation. Just as Krishna provided support and insights to the Pandavas, organizational leaders should foster mentorship programs that connect experienced individuals with younger employees. This collaboration can lead to the exchange of diverse perspectives, ultimately sparking new ideas and strategies. Encouraging cross-functional teams can also enhance creativity, allowing for a blend of skills and viewpoints that can lead to innovative solutions.

Moreover, the Mahabharata teaches the importance of ethical decision-making and integrity in leadership. Leaders who model these values create an environment of trust, enabling employees to feel secure in sharing their ideas and taking risks. When team members believe in the organization's commitment to ethical practices, they are more likely to engage wholeheartedly in innovation efforts. This alignment between values and actions fosters a sense of purpose, motivating employees to contribute their best ideas.

Another critical aspect of agility in the Mahabharata is the characters' ability to adapt to changing circumstances. The fluid nature of alliances and strategies in the epic illustrates that organizations must remain flexible and responsive to market dynamics. Leaders can cultivate this agility by promoting a mindset of continuous learning and improvement. Implementing regular feedback loops, such as retrospectives or brainstorming sessions, can help teams quickly identify areas for enhancement and adjust their strategies accordingly.

Furthermore, embracing technology and tools that facilitate collaboration can enhance both innovation and agility. In the Mahabharata, communication among the Pandavas was crucial in executing their strategies. In modern organizations, leveraging digital platforms for idea sharing, project management, and real-time communication can break down silos and foster a culture of collaboration. This interconnectedness enables faster decision-making and encourages collective problem-solving.

Finally, recognizing and celebrating innovative efforts, regardless of their outcome, is essential in building a culture of innovation. The Mahabharata's emphasis on valor and recognition can inspire organizations to acknowledge contributions that push boundaries, even when they do not lead to immediate success. Celebrating both small and large wins reinforces a culture where innovation is valued and employees feel empowered to contribute.

By drawing lessons from the Mahabharata, organizations can cultivate a culture of innovation and agility that thrives on creativity, collaboration, and ethical leadership. By fostering an environment that encourages experimentation, values mentorship, embraces flexibility, and utilizes technology, businesses can position themselves to navigate challenges and seize opportunities in a rapidly changing world.

CHAPTER NINE

❧

Sustainability

Legacy and Sustainability - The Impact beyond the Battle

In the Mahabharata, the themes of legacy and sustainability resonate powerfully, particularly in the aftermath of the devastating Kurukshetra War, where the repercussions of conflict extend far beyond the battlefield. The narrative emphasizes that the choices made by its characters have profound implications for future generations, illustrating that true legacy is not merely defined by victories or conquests, but by the values and lessons imparted to society. Following the war, the Pandavas, despite their triumph, grapple with immense guilt and the moral decay resulting from their actions, highlighting the critical need for leaders to consider the long-term effects of their decisions on the fabric of society. Yudhishthira's commitment to restoring dharma reflects an understanding that a sustainable legacy is built on ethical principles and social responsibility, urging contemporary leaders to prioritize the collective good over short-term gains. This echoes modern business practices, where organizations are increasingly recognizing the importance of sustainability, not just in environmental terms, but also in fostering community well-being and ethical governance. Furthermore, the epic encourages a reflective approach to history, where the lessons learned from past mistakes can inform future decisions, reinforcing the notion that responsible leadership must be rooted in a deep awareness of its impact on people and the environment. Ultimately, the Mahabharata serves as a poignant reminder that lasting legacy is intricately tied to the pursuit of a harmonious and sustainable future, urging leaders to act with integrity and foresight in their endeavors.

The Long-Term Vision

The concept of long-term vision is a pivotal theme in the Mahabharata, intricately woven into the fabric of its narrative and character arcs, demonstrating how foresight and strategic planning are essential for sustainable success and societal well-being. Central to this theme is the figure of Krishna, who embodies the qualities of a visionary leader, guiding the Pandavas through the complexities of the Kurukshetra War and the moral dilemmas they face. His advice often emphasizes the importance of looking beyond immediate gains, urging the Pandavas to consider the broader implications of their actions on future generations and the world around them. This perspective is particularly relevant in today's rapidly changing environment, where leaders must navigate complex challenges while remaining grounded in a clear, long-term vision. The choices made by characters like Yudhishthira and Arjuna reflect their understanding of the importance of legacy and the need to uphold dharma, or righteousness, even amidst chaos and conflict. Yudhishthira, despite his struggles and the burdens of leadership, strives to maintain integrity and justice, illustrating that true leadership involves making decisions that prioritize ethical values over fleeting victories. This commitment to a higher purpose fosters resilience and unity among the Pandavas, enabling them to work collaboratively towards a common goal that transcends individual ambitions. Furthermore, the long-term vision in the Mahabharata is underscored by the consequences faced by characters who fail to consider the future. Duryodhana's fixation on power and jealousy leads to his downfall, serving as a cautionary tale about the perils of short-sightedness and self-interest. In contrast, Krishna's strategic foresight and emphasis on collaboration illustrate the necessity of cultivating relationships and alliances to achieve lasting outcomes. The alliances formed throughout the narrative, such as the support from Bhishma and Drona, highlight the value of building a network of trust and cooperation, which is essential for realizing a shared vision. Additionally, the Mahabharata teaches that the long-term vision must be adaptable, as the dynamics of power and morality shift throughout the epic. Characters like Abhimanyu and Draupadi represent the evolving nature of leadership, showcasing that innovation and resilience are key components of effective long-term planning. Their journeys remind us that the pursuit of a visionary goal requires flexibility and the ability to navigate unforeseen challenges, further emphasizing the need for leaders to remain agile in their approach. In contemporary contexts, organizations can learn from these insights by integrating long-term thinking into their strategic frameworks, fostering a culture that values ethical decision-making, collaboration, and adaptability. By doing so, they can build sustainable practices that not only address immediate challenges but also contribute to a positive legacy that benefits future generations. Ultimately, the Mahabharata serves as a profound reminder that a successful long-term vision is rooted in ethical leadership, collaborative efforts, and a deep understanding of the interconnectedness of actions and their consequences. It encourages leaders to look beyond the present, crafting strategies that honor the past while paving the way for a just and sustainable future, thus resonating with the timeless relevance of the epic's teachings in the modern world.

What happens after the battle? Sustainability in business

After the climactic battle of Kurukshetra in the Mahabharata, the consequences of conflict extend deeply into the realm of sustainability, serving as a poignant metaphor for the challenges faced by businesses in contemporary society. The aftermath of the war reveals the profound impact of choices made during the battle, as the Pandavas grapple with the devastation that has befallen their kingdom, including immense loss of life, moral ambiguity, and the erosion of dharma, or righteousness. This scenario underscores a critical lesson for businesses: the importance of considering the long-term implications of their actions and decisions, rather than focusing solely on immediate gains or victories. Just as the Pandavas must confront the emptiness of their triumph, organizations must recognize that short-term profits achieved at the expense of ethical considerations can lead to long-lasting repercussions. The Mahabharata illustrates the necessity for sustainable practices that prioritize the welfare of all stakeholders—employees, customers, and the community—rather than a singular focus on profit maximization.

In the epic, Yudhishthira's struggle with guilt and his determination to restore balance and righteousness highlight the significance of ethical leadership in the aftermath of any major endeavor. His commitment to dharma reflects the growing recognition in today's business world that sustainability is not just an environmental concern but also a moral imperative. Leaders must strive to build organizations that embody integrity, transparency, and social responsibility, fostering a culture that values ethical practices. This approach not only cultivates trust among stakeholders but also enhances the long-term viability of the organization. The characters' reflections on their actions post-war serve as a powerful reminder of the need for continuous learning and adaptation. The lessons learned from the Kurukshetra conflict resonate with the concept of corporate sustainability, where organizations must engage in regular assessments of their practices and strategies to ensure they align with evolving societal values and environmental concerns. The Pandavas' efforts to rebuild their kingdom can be likened to businesses that seek to innovate and adapt in response to changing market dynamics and consumer expectations. This involves not only investing in sustainable technologies and practices but also nurturing a culture of innovation that encourages employees to contribute ideas for improvement and positive change.

Additionally, the epic emphasizes the importance of collaboration and collective responsibility in the aftermath of conflict. The Pandavas, though victorious, realize that their leadership must extend beyond their individual ambitions to encompass the broader needs of their people. This underscores the idea that sustainable business practices are best achieved through collaboration with various stakeholders, including suppliers, customers, and local communities. By fostering partnerships that prioritize shared goals and mutual benefits, organizations can enhance their resilience and adaptability in the face of challenges. The aftermath of the battle also highlights the significance of legacy in shaping future actions. Just as the Pandavas are left to ponder the legacy of their decisions, businesses must consider the long-term impact of their operations on the environment and society. This involves embracing corporate social responsibility initiatives that contribute positively to the community and environment, ensuring that future generations inherit a world that is healthier and more equitable. The Mahabharata teaches that legacy is not merely a product of success in the present but is intricately tied to the values and actions that define an organization over time.

The consequence of the Kurukshetra War serves as a profound metaphor for the necessity of sustainability in business. The lessons drawn from the Mahabharata emphasize the importance of ethical leadership, continuous learning, collaboration, and a commitment to legacy, urging organizations to adopt practices that not only seek immediate success but also contribute to a sustainable future. By integrating these principles into their core strategies, businesses can navigate the complexities of modern markets while fostering a culture that values integrity and responsibility. Ultimately, the teachings of the Mahabharata remind us that the true measure of success lies not just in victories won but in the enduring impact of our choices on the world around us.

Lessons on Corporate Social Responsibility

The Mahabharata offers profound insights into the concept of Corporate Social Responsibility (CSR), illustrating how ethical leadership and societal well-being are intricately linked. Throughout the epic, characters grapple with moral dilemmas that highlight the importance of acting in the best interests of their communities. A salient example is Yudhishthira, whose commitment to dharma—righteousness and ethical conduct—reflects the essence of responsible leadership. After the devastating war, he embodies the principles of CSR by prioritizing the welfare of his subjects, recognizing that true leadership extends beyond personal ambition to encompass the broader needs of society. His efforts to restore justice and rebuild the war-torn kingdom serve as a reminder that businesses today must similarly focus on the impacts of their actions, fostering a sense of accountability toward stakeholders, including employees, customers, and the community. The Mahabharata also emphasizes the significance of collaboration in achieving social responsibility; the Pandavas rely on alliances and support from others to navigate their challenges, illustrating that effective CSR requires partnerships and collective efforts. This aligns with contemporary business practices, where organizations are encouraged to engage with local communities and stakeholders to address social and environmental issues collaboratively. Additionally, the character of Draupadi, who advocates for justice and equality, highlights the importance of inclusivity in CSR initiatives, reminding us that organizations must consider diverse perspectives and address the needs of marginalized groups. The epic teaches that ethical decision-making and social responsibility are not merely adjuncts to business strategy but are essential for sustainable success and legacy. By integrating these lessons from the Mahabharata, organizations can cultivate a culture of responsibility that not only enhances their reputation but also contributes to the overall well-being of society, ultimately leading to a more equitable and sustainable future.

Aligning business goals with societal needs

Aligning business goals with societal needs is a critical theme in the Mahabharata, where the actions and decisions of its characters reveal profound insights into the importance of ethical leadership and community welfare. Central to this narrative is Yudhishthira, the eldest Pandava, whose unwavering commitment to dharma underscores the necessity for leaders to prioritize righteousness and social responsibility over personal gain. After the devastating Kurukshetra War, Yudhishthira's journey toward rebuilding the kingdom reflects a broader understanding that true success is not merely measured by victories or wealth, but by the positive impact one's actions have on society. This ethos resonates deeply with contemporary business practices, where organizations are increasingly recognizing the need to align their objectives with the expectations and values of the communities they serve.

The aftermath of the war serves as a poignant reminder that neglecting societal needs can lead to profound consequences, not only for individuals but for entire communities. Yudhishthira's struggles with guilt and his resolve to restore justice illustrate the importance of engaging with the public's needs and aspirations. Similarly, businesses today must consider how their operations affect various stakeholders, including employees, customers, and local communities. By fostering an environment where social considerations are woven into the fabric of business strategy, organizations can enhance their reputations and build lasting relationships with those they serve.

The Mahabharata also highlights the role of collaboration in achieving alignment between business goals and societal needs. The Pandavas' victories are not solely the result of individual prowess; rather, they stem from their ability to forge alliances and seek counsel from wise advisors like Krishna. This collaborative spirit emphasizes that businesses, too, should engage with diverse stakeholders to understand their needs and co-create solutions that benefit both the organization and society at large. Establishing partnerships with local communities, NGOs, and government entities can enhance a company's capacity to address social issues effectively, fostering a sense of shared responsibility that is vital for sustainable growth.

Furthermore, the character of Draupadi embodies the need for inclusivity in aligning business goals with societal needs. Her fierce advocacy for justice and equality highlights that organizations must not only focus on profitability but also ensure that their practices reflect a commitment to diversity and social equity. In today's context, this means prioritizing fair labor practices, supporting marginalized groups, and promoting gender equality within the workplace. By embracing diversity and ensuring that all voices are heard, businesses can cultivate a culture of innovation and resilience that aligns their goals with the aspirations of a broader society.

Another important lesson from the Mahabharata is the necessity of long-term thinking when aligning business goals with societal needs. The narrative teaches that immediate gains can often lead to unforeseen consequences, as seen in the character arcs of Duryodhana and others who pursue power without regard for ethical implications. In contrast, Yudhishthira's commitment to dharma and community welfare reflects the need for businesses to adopt a long-term perspective, considering how their decisions today will impact future generations. This forward-thinking approach can lead organizations to invest in sustainable practices, promote environmental stewardship, and support community development initiatives that align with societal aspirations. The Mahabharata provides valuable insights into the importance of aligning business goals with societal needs through ethical leadership, collaboration, inclusivity, and long-term thinking. By integrating these principles into their core strategies, organizations can not only enhance their reputations but also contribute meaningfully to the communities they serve. This alignment fosters trust, loyalty, and a sense of shared purpose, ultimately leading to a more sustainable and equitable future. The lessons from this epic remind us that the true measure of success lies not just in financial gains but in the lasting positive impact of our actions on society, urging leaders to act with integrity and foresight in their endeavors.

Conclusion

The Eternal Lessons of the Mahabharata

The Mahabharata resonates with timeless lessons that extend far beyond its narrative, offering profound insights applicable to various aspects of life, leadership, and societal responsibility. At its core, the epic serves as a poignant reminder of the complexities of dharma—righteousness and ethical duty—which underscores the challenges individuals face in navigating moral dilemmas. Characters like Yudhishthira exemplify the struggle between ambition and ethical integrity, illustrating that true leadership requires a commitment to justice and the well-being of others. The consequences of the Kurukshetra War poignantly highlight the repercussions of choices made in pursuit of power, urging contemporary leaders and organizations to consider the long-term impact of their actions on society. Additionally, the Mahabharata emphasizes the importance of collaboration, as seen in the alliances formed by the Pandavas and the counsel provided by Krishna, reinforcing the idea that collective efforts are crucial in achieving meaningful outcomes. This spirit of teamwork and shared purpose is vital in today's interconnected world, where solutions to complex challenges often require diverse perspectives and cooperative strategies. Furthermore, the epic underscores the significance of empathy, resilience, and adaptability, qualities that are essential for navigating the uncertainties of modern life and business. The experiences of characters like Draupadi remind us of the importance of inclusivity and the need to advocate for justice and equality in all spheres of influence. Ultimately, the Mahabharata imparts eternal lessons about the balance between personal ambition and collective responsibility, urging individuals and organizations to align their goals with the greater good. As we reflect on these teachings, we are reminded that the pursuit of dharma, ethical leadership, and a commitment to societal well-being are not merely historical ideals but essential principles for fostering a more just and sustainable future. The wisdom of the Mahabharata continues to inspire generations, encouraging us to act with integrity and foresight, ensuring that our choices contribute positively to the legacy we leave behind.

Summarizing Key Takeaways

Summarizing the key takeaways from the Mahabharata reveals a treasure trove of insights that remain remarkably relevant to contemporary life, leadership, and organizational practices. At its heart, the epic is a profound exploration of dharma, or righteousness, which serves as a guiding principle for ethical decision-making and moral responsibility. One of the most significant takeaways is the importance of integrity and the commitment to uphold ethical standards, as demonstrated by characters like Yudhishthira, who exemplifies the struggle between ambition and moral duty. His unwavering adherence to truth and justice, even in the face of overwhelming challenges, emphasizes that true leadership requires prioritizing ethical considerations over mere success or power. This principle resonates strongly in today's business environment, where the emphasis on corporate governance and ethical practices is critical for building trust with stakeholders and fostering sustainable growth.

Another essential lesson is the value of collaboration and the recognition that individual achievements are often the result of collective efforts. The alliances formed throughout the Mahabharata, particularly among the Pandavas and their supporters, highlight the necessity of teamwork and shared purpose in overcoming obstacles. This underscores the modern understanding that organizations thrive when they cultivate a culture of collaboration, encouraging diverse perspectives and harnessing the strengths of each team member. Additionally, the guidance provided by Krishna as a mentor and strategist illustrates the importance of seeking counsel and building relationships that enhance decision-making, a lesson that underscores the value of mentorship and advisory networks in contemporary leadership. The epic also delves into the complexities of human emotions and relationships, showcasing the impact of jealousy, pride, and ambition on personal and collective outcomes. Characters like Duryodhana serve as cautionary figures, demonstrating how unchecked desires can lead to ruin and suffering. This teaches that self-awareness and emotional intelligence are critical for leaders, enabling them to navigate interpersonal dynamics effectively and make decisions that consider the broader implications for their teams and communities. Moreover, the narrative emphasizes the significance of resilience and adaptability in the face of adversity. The Pandavas' ability to regroup and strategize after significant setbacks illustrates that success often requires perseverance and the willingness to learn from failure—a lesson that is vital for individuals and organizations striving to innovate and thrive in an ever-changing environment.

Inclusivity and social justice also emerge as crucial themes in the Mahabharata. Draupadi's unwavering strength and advocacy for justice highlight the importance of giving voice to the marginalized and ensuring that equity is at the forefront of decision-making. This resonates deeply with contemporary discussions on diversity and inclusion in the workplace, where organizations are increasingly recognizing the benefits of fostering an environment that values all perspectives and experiences. Furthermore, the consequences of the Kurukshetra War serve as a powerful reminder of the devastating impact of conflict and the necessity of pursuing peace and harmony within society. The aftermath of the battle compels both leaders and organizations to reflect on their actions and consider how they can contribute to the greater good, ensuring that their pursuits align with sustainable practices that benefit both present and future generations.

The Mahabharata teaches that legacy is built not only on victories but on the values and principles one leaves behind. The characters' reflections on their choices and their desire to restore balance and righteousness emphasize the importance of long-term thinking in leadership. In modern business, this translates into a commitment to Corporate Social Responsibility (CSR) and sustainable practices that prioritize the well-being of communities and the environment. By integrating ethical considerations into their core missions, organizations can foster a sense of purpose that resonates with both employees and customers, ultimately enhancing their brand reputation and long-term viability. The Mahabharata also provides an enduring framework for ethical leadership, collaboration, resilience, inclusivity, and social responsibility. The lessons drawn from its characters and narratives continue to inspire individuals and organizations to navigate the complexities of modern life with integrity and foresight. By embracing these key takeaways, leaders can foster a culture of accountability, innovation, and sustainability, ensuring that their actions contribute positively to the legacy they wish to leave behind, and paving the way for a more just and equitable future for all. The timeless wisdom of the Mahabharata invites us to reflect on our choices, understand the interconnectedness of our actions, and commit to a path that honors both our individual aspirations and our collective responsibilities.

Reflection on how ancient wisdom transforms corporate strategy

The integration of ancient wisdom, particularly drawn from the Mahabharata, into corporate strategy offers profound insights into ethics, leadership, conflict resolution, and decision-making that remain profoundly relevant in today's complex business environments. The Mahabharata, an ancient Indian epic, encapsulates deep philosophical teachings through its narratives and characters, providing a reservoir of strategic wisdom applicable to modern corporate scenarios. Central to the epic is the concept of Dharma, or moral duty, which emphasizes the importance of ethical considerations in decision-making processes. In corporate strategy, aligning business objectives with ethical practices not only enhances corporate reputation but also fosters sustainable success that benefits all stakeholders, contrary to the short-term, profit-driven motives often observed in contemporary business practices. This philosophical underpinning suggests that corporations should not just pursue profitability but also embrace responsibilities toward society and the environment, reminiscent of the principles of Raj Dharma outlined in the epic, which govern the conduct of leaders and rulers. The character of Arjuna exemplifies the struggle between adhering to personal ethics versus corporate pressures, providing a critical reflection point for business leaders today as they navigate corporate governance and social responsibilities amid competitive landscapes. Additionally, the Mahabharata illustrates various forms of conflict resolution, whether through diplomacy, dialogue, or strategic warfare, offering a multitude of approaches that corporate leaders can adopt while managing internal and external conflicts. The principles of negotiation seen in the epic, especially in the context of the Kurukshetra War, reflect the importance of understanding the adversary and oneself, teaching contemporary executives the value of emotional intelligence and the necessity of strategic foresight in negotiations. Moreover, the insights on leadership, as demonstrated through the dynamic roles of characters like Krishna, who embodies wisdom and guidance, highlight the quintessential attributes of visionary leadership that modern organizations require in an increasingly volatile market landscape. Companies can harness transformational leadership by encouraging a culture that prioritizes learning, adaptability, and resilience, principles that resonate deeply within the vast tapestry of the Mahabharata. Furthermore, the epic underscores the significance of long-term strategic thinking as exemplified in various plot arcs, reminding corporate strategists that enduring success is often the result of considered, strategic actions rather than reactive, short-sighted maneuvers. The narratives also explore the consequences of hubris and moral failure, serving as cautionary tales for modern enterprises that may overlook ethical standards in their pursuit of growth. By reflecting on the lessons embedded within the Mahabharata, organizations can cultivate a corporate ethos that emphasizes ethical decision-making, holistic leadership, and conflict resolution strategies that enhance their strategic frameworks. This approach not only fosters a sustainable corporate identity and strong stakeholder relationships but also aligns the organization with larger societal goals, thereby transforming typical corporate strategies into more meaningful, impactful practices that draw upon the wisdom of ages past to navigate the challenges of the present. Thus, embracing the timeless teachings of the Mahabharata allows businesses to not only thrive in a competitive environment but also contribute positively to the society and environment in which they operate, ensuring that their legacy is one of honor, integrity, and social responsibility, much like the heroes and lessons that the epic immortalizes.

Looking Ahead

Looking ahead, the ancient Indian epic, the Mahabharata, offers profound insights that resonate with contemporary dilemmas, providing guidance for navigating future challenges in both personal and collective contexts. At its core, the Mahabharata illustrates the complexity of human relationships and the moral intricacies that arise in times of turmoil, reflecting the ongoing struggles we face in modern society. The narrative surrounding the Kurukshetra War serves as a powerful allegory for the conflicts inherent in organizational dynamics and national governance, emphasizing the necessity for ethical decision-making. As we contemplate our future, the lessons from the Mahabharata remind us of the importance of Dharma, or righteous duty, pushing us to consider the implications of our choices not just on ourselves but on the broader community. Characters such as Yudhishthira exemplify the balance of integrity and responsibility, urging future leaders to cultivate virtues of honesty and accountability, especially when faced with moral dilemmas that require difficult choices. Furthermore, the interactions between Arjuna and Krishna illuminate the significance of dialogue and counsel in leadership; Arjuna's hesitations and Krishna's guidance underscore the necessity of seeking wisdom in uncertainty, encouraging a collaborative approach to problem-solving in both corporate and social frameworks. As we look to reconcile technological advancements with ethical responsibilities, the Mahabharata's reflections on the consequences of ambition and desire, as depicted in the downfall of characters like Duryodhana, serve as a critical reminder to prioritize sustainable practices over short-term gains. The theme of foresight is prevalent throughout the text, particularly in how characters plan their actions amidst the unseen consequences of their decisions, urging modern strategists to cultivate a mindset that embraces long-term thinking. The epic also teaches us about the importance of alliances and the fluctuating nature of loyalty, reminding us to build relationships based on trust and mutual respect as we forge ahead in an increasingly interconnected world. By integrating these timeless teachings into our societal practices, we can foster a culture that values cooperation, ethical standards, and compassionate leadership, thereby transforming potential conflicts into opportunities for growth and collaboration. The Mahabharata ultimately encourages a forward-looking perspective that inherently appreciates diversity, advocating for understanding and embracing different viewpoints, which is crucial as we address the multifaceted global challenges that lie ahead. Embracing the wisdom of the Mahabharata not only illuminates our path towards a more equitable and sustainable future but also serves as an enduring source of inspiration that reinforces the moral fabric of our collective aspirations while guiding us through the moral complexities and choices we will encounter in our journey forward.

How businesses can implement these lessons in the modern world

Implementing the timeless lessons from the Mahabharata into modern business practices involves a multi-faceted approach that integrates ethical conduct, strategic foresight, and a deep understanding of human relationships, all of which are crucial for building sustainable organizations in today's dynamic environment. The Mahabharata, a rich tapestry of narratives, moral dilemmas, and philosophical discourse, provides invaluable insights into leadership, conflict resolution, and the importance of adhering to Dharma, or righteous duty, which can serve as a guiding principle for contemporary businesses seeking to navigate ethical challenges and social responsibilities. One of the core lessons from the epic is the significance of ethical leadership, as embodied by characters such as Yudhishthira, whose commitment to truth and righteousness often placed him at odds with more expedient but morally questionable choices. Modern businesses can implement this lesson by fostering a corporate culture that prioritizes ethical behavior over short-term gains, encouraging leaders to make decisions that reflect integrity and transparency, thus building a trustworthy reputation among stakeholders. Additionally, the concept of Dharma can be extended to corporate social responsibility (CSR), where businesses are called to contribute positively to society, ensuring their operations not only benefit shareholders but also the community and environment. This holistic approach can lead to long-term sustainability, as organizations that embrace CSR are increasingly favored by consumers who seek to support businesses aligned with their values. Furthermore, the characters of Krishna and Arjuna embody the essence of mentorship and guidance, highlighting the role of wise counsel in effective leadership. Businesses today can implement this lesson by promoting mentorship programs within their organizations, allowing experienced leaders to guide younger professionals in navigating the complexities of their roles, thereby enhancing decision-making capabilities and fostering a culture of continuous learning. Moreover, the Mahabharata teaches us the importance of understanding diverse perspectives and the art of negotiation, as exemplified by Krishna's diplomatic engagements during the peace negotiations before the war. Modern organizations can adopt these lessons by embracing diversity and inclusion within their teams, recognizing that a variety of viewpoints can lead to more innovative solutions and improved problem-solving. This can also manifest in fostering collaborative environments where negotiation and dialogue are encouraged as primary tools for conflict resolution and team dynamics. The epic also emphasizes the need for foresight and strategic planning, as seen in the meticulous preparations of both the Pandavas and Kauravas leading up to the Kurukshetra War. Today's businesses can incorporate this insight by adopting strategic frameworks that prioritize long-term planning and risk assessment, rather than merely reacting to immediate challenges. Establishing a robust risk management strategy enables organizations to anticipate potential issues and respond effectively, much like the various strategies employed during the war, which included alliances, intelligence gathering, and adaptive tactics. Additionally, the theme of kinship and loyalty, so evident in the relationships between the Pandavas and their allies, serves as a reminder of the importance of cultivating strong relationships with employees, customers, and partners. Businesses can implement this by creating a loyal organizational culture that values relationships, fosters teamwork, and recognizes individual contributions. Engaging employees through recognition programs and fostering a sense of belonging can significantly enhance morale and productivity, creating an environment where individuals feel valued and motivated to contribute to the organization's success. The epic's exploration of crises, particularly the moral and ethical crises faced by characters like Arjuna, teaches modern leaders the necessity of maintaining composure under pressure and making decisions grounded in ethical clarity. Companies can implement training programs focused on developing emotional intelligence and ethical decision-making skills, preparing their leaders to face crises with resilience and integrity. By encouraging a culture of ethical reflection and collective problem-solving during crises, organizations can emerge stronger and more cohesive. Additionally, the Mahabharata illustrates the consequences of unchecked ambition and ego, as embodied by characters like Duryodhana, whose hubris ultimately leads to downfall. Businesses today can learn from this by instilling frameworks that promote humility, accountability, and a team-oriented approach to success, thus mitigating the risks associated with individualism and excessive competition. Implementing feedback mechanisms that encourage open communication and continuous improvement can help foster a sense of collective ownership and responsibility, countering the detrimental effects of siloed thinking and rivalry. In terms of operations and strategies, the Mahabharata also highlights the wisdom of patience and perseverance, particularly in the face of adversity. Organizations can adopt this principle by cultivating a growth mindset among employees, encouraging them to view challenges as opportunities for learning and development. This approach can be supported by providing resources for professional growth and resilience training, showcasing that enduring success often comes from sustained effort rather than immediate results. Finally, the Mahabharata emphasizes the value of legacy, both in terms of the impact one leaves on society and the narratives that shape collective memory. Modern businesses can implement this lesson by recognizing their role in the broader context of societal development, engaging in initiatives that promote social welfare, environmental stewardship, and ethical governance. By embedding these values into their core missions, organizations can build lasting legacies that not only enhance their reputations but also contribute meaningfully to the fabric of society. To summarize, the Mahabharata is not merely an ancient text but a source of wisdom that remains relevant for contemporary business practices. By integrating its lessons on ethical leadership, strategic foresight, relationship building, and an uncompromising commitment to moral principles into their operational frameworks, modern businesses can navigate the complexities of today's market landscape while contributing to a more equitable, sustainable, and harmonious society. The epic serves as a reminder that the path to success is not solely measured by profit margins or shareholder value but also by the ethical considerations and societal impacts of one's actions, ultimately guiding businesses toward a future where moral integrity and corporate responsibility are at the forefront of strategic decision-making. In doing so, organizations not only honor the wisdom of the past but also position themselves to thrive amid the challenges and uncertainties of the modern world, ensuring that their legacies are marked by integrity, social impact, and enduring contributions to the communities they serve.

Bibliography

- Achieving Environmental Harmony: An Analysis Based on the Narratives From Mahabharata. 2023.
- Angel Kwolek-Folland. Engendering Business: Men and Women in the Corporate Office, 1870–1930. Baltimore: Johns Hopkins University Press, 1994.
- Bharadwaj, R. L. The Mahabharata Patriline: Gender, Culture, and the Royal Hereditary. 2009.
- Charles E. Freedeman. The Triumph of Corporate Capitalism in France, 1867–1914. Rochester, N.Y.: University of Rochester Press, 1993.
- Charlie Whitham. Post-War Business Planners in the United States, 1939–48: The Rise of the Corporate Moderates. New York: Bloomsbury Academic, 2016.
- David S. Allen. Democracy, Inc.: The Press and Law in the Corporate Rationalization of the Public Sphere. 2005.
- Eckehard F. Rosenbaum, Frank Bönker, Hans-Jürgen Wagener (eds.). Privatization, Corporate Governance and the Emergence of Markets. Studies in Economic Transition. New York: St. Martin's Press, 2000.
- Gustavo Flores-Macías. Contemporary State Building: Elite Taxation and Public Safety in Latin America. New York: Cambridge University Press, 2022
- J.E. Parkinson. Corporate Power and Responsibility: Issues in the Theory of Company Law. Oxford: Clarendon Press, 1993.
- Language Model Based Related Word Prediction from an Indian Epic - Mahabharata. 2022.
- M. J. Whincop. An Economic and Jurisprudential Genealogy of Corporate Law. Aldershot: Ashgate, 2001.
- Mishra, Akhilesh. Epic Nation: Reimagining the Mahabharata in the Age of the Empire. 2009.
- Rāmopākhyāna: The Story of Rāma in the Mahābhārata: An Independent-Study Reader in Sanskrit. 2003.
- The making of womanhood: gender relations in the Mahābhārata. 2012
- Vora, Dhairyabala P. Evolution of Morals in the Epics (Mahābhārata and Rāmāyaṇa). Bombay: Popular Bookdepot, 1959.
- W. Carl Kester. Japanese Takeovers: The Global Contest for Corporate Control. Boston, Mass.: Harvard Business School Press, 1990
- Yoga: The Indian Tradition. John Brockington, et al. (2003).

Milton Keynes UK
Ingram Content Group UK Ltd.
UKHW050122231124
451130UK00022B/93

9 798896 101512